JOURNEY

The Gift of Being a Psychic Medium

Lisa Andres

Cover Design by Regina Wamba
http://www.maeidesign.com

Editing by Patrick and April Durham
http://editingandebooks.com

ISBN: 978-1-7320375-1-9

ACKNOWLEDGEMENTS

Carol Westphal, for assistance with the wording of the subtitle *(The Gift of Being A Psychic Medium)*

To all my family, friends, loved ones, teachers, clients and more that have supported me through my journey as a psychic medium: I have profound gratitude.

LISA ANDRES

CONTENTS

LISA ANDRES

INTRODUCTION

I've been a medium all my life, knowing since I was a young girl in the mid-1970s that I could see and sense Spirit. At the time, it terrified me.

I quickly learned that my Roman Catholic family did not understand that I was seeing spirits, and they sent me to a psychiatrist that told me the boogie man wasn't real. I kept quiet after that, but I spent a lot of my early childhood years either with my head under the covers or standing on my bed in the middle of the night because I could feel all the spirits around me and felt scared.

As I grew older, life took over, and my gift didn't come back into play until I was about 17 years old. I started to sense paranormal activity. I remember my friend Kim and I used to drive around a lake near the city of Minneapolis, looking at the big houses. One night we saw what we thought was a spirit in the window of one home, a woman with a flowing gown that seemed to be floating. We both screamed and stepped on the gas to get out of there as quickly as possible.

As two teenage girls would do, we went back to her house, discussed it, and drove by that house a night or two later. The spirit wasn't there. We were both disappointed and relieved. A few nights later, we were driving by and there she was again, this transparent lady that seemed to be floating. We screamed again. We occasionally discuss that experience to this day.

After I moved into my first apartment, I started to open up, which meant the paranormal activity around me seemed overwhelming. I could hear voices, felt like I was being touched or having my hair pulled (when nothing was there) when I was sleeping, and occasionally saw things moving. I kept trying to figure out how to turn it off. I knew I wasn't crazy, and I knew it was Spirit. I also knew I wanted nothing to do with it.

I spent the next 10 or so years living life, and the paranormal activity persisted but not to as great an extent. At this point, I think that I may have just gotten used to it. I used to tell the spirits that followed me around that if they wanted me to do something for them or listen to them, they had to respect "human business hours" and not wake me up in the middle of the night. That approach wasn't too effective.

My maternal grandmother, Ali, was rather ahead of her time when it came to being New Age. She and I talked about a lot of what was happening to me, and I think that's what helped me through those days. She kept asking me to go with her to see a psychic. I usually said no, but one night I wanted to get out of the house and went. The psychic told me I was a medium.

Not long afterwards, another medium also told me I was a medium, and there was always Grandma Ali telling me that, too. It wasn't until I was in my mid-thirties that I finally threw my hands up in frustration because I could not turn off my capacity to sense, see, and feel Spirit. I went to a psychic development class to see if I could learn anything that would help me.

In that class, I learned about all the psychic senses, but there wasn't too much for mediums specifically. I wanted to find a class specific to mediums after that, and I asked the universe to help me find the right teacher. I then landed in another class that cost a lot of money but was worth every penny. Somehow, the universe magically supplied me with the resources I needed to get to that class, and I knew after that I didn't want to just go home and try to pretend it had never happened.

Six months later, after I'd also attended my first class for medium development, I asked a friend if I could do free readings at an event she was hosting, and she agreed. I did so many readings that first day I didn't have time to be nervous. I also learned that day that mediums were also psychics because I thought that all my clients would be asking me to connect with Spirit, but my very first client asked about an item that was missing, which is a psychic question (a question having to do with life advice). I decided then that I would just trust what I saw clairvoyantly, and I delivered the information about where I thought the object she was missing would be. After that, I embraced that mediums are also psychics.

The rest, as they say, is history. That was 2009. I have been doing readings, both as a medium and as a psychic, ever since. I'm not a full-time medium at the time of the writing this book, but I do many private readings. A good many of them are at psychic fairs or expos where I do back-to-back mini-readings. I've also done platform readings, which are also called demonstration-style mediumship, a handful of times. I want to do this more and trust that when it's time, I will be called to do so.

In 2013, I felt it was time for another teacher, and I went to my first class with a different, well-known medium. I saw that same teacher again in 2014 when he taught a different class with another well-respected medium. Both times he talked about Stansted, also known as the Arthur Findlay College. (http://www.arthurfindlaycollege.org/) The way it was spoken of made it seem like a challenge and a good development opportunity. I started asking questions about it and thought that I would go when the time was right and I was ready, as the class schedule sounded very intense to me.

I went to Arthur Findlay College for the first time in 2015, and then again in 2016. I will likely continue to go there every couple of years to keep up with my own development as a medium. I remember that one teacher said, "When I finally accepted that I was a medium, I accepted that I wanted to be the best that I could be." That has always reminded me to strive to be better at this gift that I have.

In 2012, I had a prophetic dream that told me to write a book. It was a near-death experience dream that felt very real. As I was following the proverbial white light, I said that I wasn't ready to leave yet. I heard a very loud, authoritative voice say: "Then WRITE THE BOOK." That book ended up being *Gifted – A Guide for Mediums, Psychics & Intuitives*.

Since I wrote that book, I've been asked to write another book like that, but I did not want to force it or write the same book twice. Although it took several years, these things guided me as I wrote this new book. This work is authentic, and that's what I want my books to be. After reading this book, you may want more information on giving readings, protection and clearing, self-care, and your spiritual team. You can find more on that information in *Gifted*.

In this book, you will find more information for both mediums and psychics. I will no longer be using the word "intuitive," but anything I direct towards psychics can also be directed towards those that consider themselves intuitive. The information in this book is intended for all levels of mediums and psychics. Some portions of the book will have encouragement and insight for beginners, and some of it is directed towards those already working with the public doing readings.

As you read this book and embrace the journey you are on as a medium, the best thing to remember is that you do not have to be like any other medium but you. The gift of being a psychic medium is a talent, and, like any talent, it has to be developed.

LISA ANDRES

CHAPTER 1: THE DIFFERENCE BETWEEN A MEDIUM AND A PSYCHIC

I am both a psychic and a medium. I had no idea I was both until I started to do readings for the first time. I thought I was only a medium, but then my first client asked me a psychic question instead of a question about a person that had passed. I was so surprised that I had no choice but to tell the client the information I was receiving at the time, which actually answered the psychic question. After that, I learned that mediums are also psychics.

I tell many new mediums that the best thing they can do is learn how to use some of their psychic skills before they try to connect with those who are deceased. New mediums don't have to do it that way, but, for me, it helped because by the time I got to trying to link with the deceased, I was a little more familiar with things like clairvoyance (the ability to "see" things psychically).

Generally speaking, all mediums are psychics, but not all psychics are mediums. That means that psychics may sometimes have deceased people come through in their readings, but the information tends to be more general. A medium can connect with the deceased person and not only receive evidence from them, but also possibly imitate their mannerisms, accents or more. That is called a link.

I know at this point that what a link is may be as clear as mud, but let me give you another example. I love pets, and my love for pets allows me to connect with the deceased in a special way. I have had many, many deceased people come through with dogs, cats, horses, or other animals as evidence of who they are or who they are trying to communicate with. When I receive that kind of information, I usually get a picture of the animal and may be able to describe what color it was or something to that effect. A pet communicator (which I am not) would be able to tell a client what the animal was thinking or feeling, but that is not information I receive. I get pet information when the deceased person brings it through as evidence, and that's all.

You don't have to know right now whether you are a psychic, a medium, or both. You may evolve from one into the other, or you may just have a knowing that you are a medium, like I always did. My thought is that if you think you are or picked up this book, you probably are one or both. You may call yourself something else – just medium or just psychic—but for all practical purposes, psychic medium is what I call myself, so that's the term I'll gravitate to during this book.

The hard part about your revelation that you are a psychic medium is having the confidence to move forward, and that is what this book can help with. Even if you already have an existing practice of demonstrating or doing private sittings, this book will help you keep moving forward with your journey.

CHAPTER 2: THE DIFFERENT LEVELS OF DEVELOPMENT

There are different levels to being a psychic medium: beginning, intermediate, and advanced. I believe that mediums are born mediums, and we all have a choice whether to develop or pay attention to that gift. I also believe the same thing about being psychic. By working to develop these gifts, you can move from the beginning medium to the intermediate or advanced medium.

I have heard many people who come to me for readings state that "everyone is a little bit psychic." Quite frankly, I am not sure I believe that. I think we all have our own intuition, but beyond that, not everyone has this gift or the ability to develop it.

Let me give you an example. My first love is music. I've always been a musician. When I realized I could play piano, I thought I would also try the guitar. My thinking was that not only was the guitar cool, but it was also a "voice" instrument like the piano. I also thought it would be relatively easy for me since I knew music theory. Boy, was I wrong. Learning it was frustrating for me, and once I was around other guitar players, I had the realization that the best I could ever be was a rhythm guitarist (the person that backs up the lead guitarist), and that was only if I tried really hard.

If we are not all born guitar players, we are also not all born psychic mediums. It just is what it is. Those of us that are born this way were born to be different. We were also born to a lifetime of service to others because that's the nature of this work.

The Beginning Level

If you feel like you can't control the spirit activity around you and are trying to figure out what it means, you are opening up as a medium or psychic. You have yet to develop this skill, which is why you feel you can't control it or why you may be afraid of it.

When I first started to open up in my early twenties, driving past a place that seemed haunted or thinking I saw or sensed a spirit scared me. Sometimes I could hear voices all around me. Luckily, instead of thinking I was totally nuts, I realized it was spirit activity. At the same time, I did not know how to turn it off. Now I know that as a psychic medium, I tend to attract spirits—we all do. Back then, I had times when I knew there were spirits in my apartment, and I would put baking soda in a pan, poor rubbing alcohol on it, light it on fire, and walk around my apartment with the flaming mixture trying to clear the energy. Oh, what a fire hazard!

In my mid-twenties, I still could not figure out how to turn off the spirits I sensed or heard. I spent a lot of time trying to create boundaries with the ghosts or spirits that knew I could communicate with, even though I did not yet communicate with them willingly. I tried to tell them not to wake me up, not to approach me, and so on. It didn't work. I did a lot of yelling at them in those days, thinking I could somehow control it.

I've never met a psychic medium who has tried not to be one and was very successful.

The Intermediate Level

When I finally started to develop as a psychic medium through my first psychic development class, it got a little better. Or it got at least a little less scary. I was a frustrated student, wanting to learn but not learning quickly enough. We did enough practice that I started to be able to somewhat tune out the noise. I also think that the spirits may have stopped bugging me because I was finally trying to figure out how to hear them. During that time, the overwhelming spirit activity was hit or miss, meaning sometimes it was overwhelming and sometimes it was peaceful.

If you have started to use your craft of doing readings or sittings, then you likely are in the advanced stage of development. If you have been studying for a while, then it's probably getting a bit better for you but may still be overwhelming at times.

The Advanced Level

Now, several years into my journey, I feel like I have an internal switch. I only turn it "on" when I am asked to do a reading. I trust that it will turn on when I have the intention of doing a reading or am standing in the power of Spirit and then turn off when I'm done linking with Spirit or doing the reading.

Have you ever heard of exercises that some psychics do to shut you down? In these exercises, the psychic meditates and asks the angels to shut you down or something to that effect. One of my teachers does an exercise where you imagine that there is a zipper that zips and unzips when you are open or closed to doing a reading. I recommend that, for the most part, you don't need to do anything ceremonious like that to shut down. The best way to shut down is to simply respect your body. For example, I don't schedule a big night out after a day of doing readings because usually I come home exhausted or tired. I come home, eat a meal, and go to bed.

Just because I shut down does not mean that I'm immune to spirit activity. I occasionally sense a spirit or feel a certain energy that I want cleared, meaning that I want the energy cleared from my space, but I no longer try to understand or explore as I would have when I first started doing readings. I just clear it, or ask my angels to help me do so, and move on. I believe that the people or energies I'm supposed to connect with come to me in formal readings.

I do not tune into people or the spirits/energy around them without their permission. So, if you are one of my friends that previously didn't know I have this gift of being a psychic medium, you are safe with me. I have good boundaries, both as a person and as a psychic medium.

I suggest that you also consider the boundaries you want to establish as a psychic medium. Do you want to walk up to strangers and read them? If you do, please ask their permission by saying something such as "Do you want this information?" Please also consider how you might feel if someone read you without your permission. I was teaching a class where a student said that she told a co-worker that someone the coworker knew was going to die within the next six months. How would you feel if someone said that to you? Wouldn't you be in a constant state of worry for the next six months? In this chapter, we talked about how your gift will become easier to control as you progress on your journey of development, but it is also important to have solid boundaries of when it is and when it is not appropriate to read people.

CHAPTER 3: PSYCHIC READINGS, GENERAL READINGS, AND PRIVATE SITTINGS

There are several types of readings that you will encounter as a psychic medium. These include psychic readings, general readings, private sittings, medium readings, and public demonstrations. The next several chapters will cover the various types of readings and what you can expect in them based on my experience. At this time, the majority of my readings are private sittings, and that's where the majority of my stories and things that I've learned have evolved from.

Psychic Readings

Let's face it, a lot of the business most of us do is with information related to the living. We all need life advice, and that may be what your client wants. In short, that's a psychic reading. Psychic readings usually talk about the following:
- Love
- Purpose

- Career
- Health

Psychic Readings – How I Do Them

In doing psychic readings, I'm always amazed at how much the reading can sometimes mirror my own life. Right now, I do a limited number of private readings in my home over the phone, and I just finished an hour reading prior to writing this. I have been personally thinking a lot lately about becoming self-employed and starting my own spiritually-based business doing readings. Right before my phone reading started, I took out one of my books about opening a spiritually-based business and set it on the coffee table for reading at a later point.

The minute the reading started, my client asked me about her career. I said, "Something tells me you have been thinking about starting your own spiritually-based business."

I said this because I had looked right at the book when she had asked me the question.

As the reading continued, there were so many things that were parallel to my own experiences. I had just put a cat to sleep and gotten a new cat; she'd just put a dog to sleep and had a new puppy. I am grieving about the cat I lost, and it was something I was connected with because I had just been crying about my deceased cat last night and the new cat was by me during the reading. I heard: "She put a dog to sleep." So, I said, "Did you recently have to put a dog to sleep?"

She started crying saying she'd done so a few months earlier and had just gotten a new puppy.

My own experience allowed me to go on about the guilt she was feeling and how she didn't want to love that new puppy because no one could replace her old dog. I explained to her that the new dog would help her heal her grief. I also knew for a fact that her deceased dog was helping with this healing process and that, somehow, he had helped name the new dog, which she confirmed.

During this reading, I discovered that I was correct about my original statement about her career path because I learned that she wanted to build her own spiritual practice doing readings and had just started in psychic development classes, which is how I started. She had so many questions, and I realized it would be so interesting if I could just explain that I trusted all the things that I got in my head to talk about during the reading, such as my own pet's death or displeasure at my job, and applied it to things I was getting about her. I trusted that it was her issue, too, which held true for most of the reading.

Readings are not always like that, but you have to remember that part of the reason that you attract the clients that you do is that their experiences sometimes mirror your own. This is true more often than not. Don't get me wrong. You will be stretched to learn new things along the way, which we'll talk about more in this book, but so many of the things you will talk to clients about draw on your own experiences, including pain and trauma, that your clients have also experienced.

When I do readings, sometimes it is me talking, and sometimes it is "them" talking. "Them" I equate to my client's spiritual team, or guides. I facilitate because I'm open to it, so I may often say "they say" when it's in the space of a psychic reading. The cadence of my voice changes slightly and things like the word "we" come out when they talk, and I know it's them. I don't even feel it, but I hear it and so does my client, so sometimes I explain who the message is coming from.

Please get over your fear of your client's spiritual team taking over during the reading and channeling through you right now. I ask for protection in all that I do, especially during readings, and you should, too. Perhaps you've heard about others that have had bad experiences with channeling; let's hope they learned from it because it's not your place to learn from it. I channel only from a place of love and believe it's usually angels or a higher power when they speak in a certain cadence through me and all the sentences are in the "we" format. You don't have to do anything you don't want to do. I just let my ability to channel evolve naturally, and if you choose not to channel, or may not be able to do so, it is okay.

Let me give you an example of channeling from my own practice. I had a client the other day who wanted to know about her love life. Basically, she had a relationship she had been waffling over for several years, had recently decided she really wanted to commit, and now wanted to know when the next step was (aka marriage). Her guides really laid into her—in a nice way—but it was no wonder that she had come to me.

Her guides ended up telling her the honest truth that she was not yet ready for marriage and needed to show her commitment to the man she'd been hurting by not being sure all those years. She said to me (and her guides as she did so), "But I have been doing that."

I (they) replied, "Ten days does not make up for seven years. You will have to be patient."

The reading went on with much more information for her that was very direct. I almost felt guilty giving it, but it was not my right to judge the information her guides were channeling through me. She thanked me in the end and said she needed to hear the information that I had relayed to her.

Remember, sometimes our job is to give the client what they need, not what they want.

General Readings

You may have a client who wants to ask a question but he or she may not be comfortable doing so. That's when a general reading comes in. Basically, that means the client wants whatever is there. He or she might say, "I want to know whatever I'm supposed to hear."

These used to—and, honestly, sometimes still do—frustrate me, but readings like this push us as psychic mediums. I learned in my advanced classes that readings like this are really the way it should be done. We go in and let Spirit do the work. If they need a psychic life reading, it will evolve, and also with the medium reading, it will evolve. Sometimes the client doesn't even know what he or she wants to know or doesn't know what to expect. Sometimes readings like this often have matters of the heart come out because many clients might be uncomfortable sitting down and saying, "Should I leave my husband?" or "When will I find love?"

Recently, I had someone come to me who wanted a general reading. I started with psychic information, but the client could not validate much of it. At first, there was a moment of doubt on the client's part, and then I realized that Spirit must be trying to come through because nothing was coming through on a psychic level. That was not only what happened, but what the client had wanted all along. She'd wanted to talk to her deceased loved ones, particularly the one that came through, and it was me trying to control where the information went that had made the reading difficult. Spirit wouldn't let me get away with that for very long, and that was a learning experience for me. So, if a client sits down and says he or she doesn't have questions, it could be a blessing in disguise and an opportunity to provide the client with information he or she wanted to ask but didn't know how to do so.

If your client has to tell you the whole story up front, or even after the reading, you're not doing your job. The more you develop, the more you will learn this.

Private Sittings

Private sittings are normally one-on-one with a client. A lot of my readings are private sittings. The ones I do at home are over the phone, but they can be done via Skype or in person. The majority of my in-person readings are when I'm out doing a psychic fair or event.

Sometimes you will really connect with a client that gives you verification by nodding his or her head, acknowledging what you are saying is correct, crying, and so forth. Other times, you may have people that are completely stoic, but that doesn't necessarily mean that the client is not feeling the same way as a person that expresses feelings more freely.

Recently, I had two friends that came to me for a reading at an event I did. They wanted to sit together, and the first woman said she didn't have any questions. I immediately connected to many details of her life, including the tragic loss of a baby. She validated me the entire way through the reading, and I think I connected with her energy so well because we had similar energy.

Then it was the second friend's turn to sit down, and there was a similar experience with her. At the end of the readings, I told them how much I really connected with them and that I'd definitely remember them. They told me they'd picked me because my energy seemed a lot like theirs. That probably not only meant they were to come to me, but that they got the information they needed because of it.

At that same show, I had one man sit down that had never had any type of reading. I remember when he wrote his name down on my sign-up sheet to book a time that I thought, "He's going to want to connect with the other side because he's got a dead mother."

When he came back for his reading, it was not his mother who was deceased, but his father. Because this man had never had a reading, it was hard for him to validate everything I said, either because he didn't connect with it or couldn't remember if what I was saying was true because of his surprise at the information that was flowing through. I thought the reading wasn't going that great, and then I saw some tears in his eyes. That helped me know that we were on the right track.

Developing Your Own Style

Recently, I did a reading for a beginning level medium. She wanted to know if she really was a medium, partly because she had seen what I did during a public demonstration and had decided that she wasn't at that level or that good. As such, she wondered if she was off course. I asked her if I inspired her, and she verified that. I then asked her how long she'd been doing work as a medium. She said she had only been doing it for six months. I explained to her that I had been doing this type of work for many years and not only had that given me practice, but I'd also studied with wonderful teachers along the way. I told her that I love it when I am inspired by other mediums because it makes me want to be a better medium and that I was glad that she, too, had been inspired because it would help her want to move forward.

As we continued the reading, she compared herself to me, especially to how I delivered the information so quickly and clearly. I said, "Well, I do my readings a lot like I am in life. What that means is I talk fast and am usually pretty to the point. So, unless that is part of your personality, you might not do exactly what I do. No two mediums are alike."

Whether you are a beginner or an advanced psychic medium, no two of us have the same voice or style. That's what makes us beautiful. Try to let other readers inspire you, but try not to be too hard on yourself if you don't think you're as good as them. You are just different and may not be as experienced as that person. As with anything, being a psychic medium is a talent. It has to be developed. At some point on my journey, I decided I wanted to expand my skills and be the best I can be in order to assist others. Hopefully, you will do the same.

It's Time to Cut the Rainbows and Unicorns

There are many practitioners that work with things of the more esoteric realm, and I even wrote a bit about this subject in *Gifted*. The more that I evolve, the more my readings do. I want them to be authentic. As a client, not only do I resonate less with the "higher level meaning" of everything, just like anyone, I want to hear the real answer not the esoteric one.

The more you do readings, the more you should be able to stretch yourself to go beyond the esoteric side of things, particularly as a medium. Think about the people that you really respect in this business. They are usually pretty accurate with evidence and that usually doesn't include fluff.

If you push yourself to go deeper and say the things that you are getting from Spirit and risk getting a "No" from your client, then you are going to get better and better at this work.

I believe that I do my readings a lot like the way I am in real life. I get straight to the point of things. I don't sugarcoat things, but I try to be as kind as possible when delivering that kind of information.

It was really difficult when a client who is a mother came to me and asked if her son was going to recover from his addiction and I had to tell her that the information I was receiving was that he wouldn't. I also gave her the other truths that came through, that he'll go to jail again and receive a felony charge. She explained to me that he already had one and that he also was saying and doing all the right things in his court-ordered treatment. I said, "I hear you, but addicts are the best liars and manipulators."

That client didn't get what she wanted, but she got what she needed. It was not my job to sugarcoat the information I was receiving, no matter how hard it was to deliver.

CHAPTER 4 – MEDIUM READINGS

Before we discuss medium readings, let me reiterate this: I have never met a medium who has tried NOT to be a medium and was very successful. The ones that try to run from it never seem to get far away enough because they always sense the dead, and those spirits know it. That's not meant to be scary; it is just true. The good news is that, based on my experience, being a medium becomes less and less scary the more you learn about it.

Medium readings are when we link with someone's that deceased. As a medium, we are typically able to pick up many details and, at times, even speak with a deceased person's likeness when we do a reading. We are able to create an actual link with the spirit that has passed. Sometimes, the spirit will even come to us before we know who we're going to talk to or what we're going to talk about.

There's no right way or wrong way to do a reading. Most of you have been doing them half your life and just don't know it. All those things that you thought that you were imagining about the spirit in the room or the thing you caught out of the corner of your eye were probably true.

No two mediums read alike. We all have different gifts or ways of bringing through information. Recently, I was with a friend that is a budding medium, and she told me that she kept seeing "Celiac" being typed out in front of her when I was asked by a woman about her grandson's allergies. My friend said that was the information she received while I was doing a demonstration and again once the medium readings were over. I didn't get that word per se, but I also don't read that way.

When I found out my friend could see words being typed out in front of her, I got really excited for her. I told her that once upon a time I had tried to tell my guides I only wanted to see words and numbers. That didn't really work out for me because we all have different gifts. My readings are primarily clairvoyant (seeing pictures) and clairsentient (sensing things about the deceased). What is interesting is that while my friend saw the word, I saw pictures.

One of my teachers once told me that there was a medium who was once a postman, so he could call out addresses. I doubt anyone else but someone who had that experience in real life could do that sort of thing. Your gift will emerge in its own way, just as mine, my friend's, and the postman's did.

To any beginning medium with no training who is looking to evolve, I would highly recommend starting with some psychic development exercises or classes. Since mediums are also psychic, it's helpful to learn what tools are in your proverbial chest of psychic gifts. That will help you when you first learn to bring through a spirit. There's so many different ways to read, but when you start, you will learn what's right for you.

When I started in my first psychic development class in 2007, I actually said to my guides that I wanted to experience only words and numbers, as I stated earlier. I acted as if I had control over this gift, but shortly after that, I learned that I did not. In my psychic development class, I started to develop my clairvoyance, or the ability to see things through my abilities. This was certainly not by choice, mind you. Every time we had to practice readings with each other, I started to see pictures in my mind. At first, it hurt. The spot in the middle of the forehead often referred to as the "third eye" throbbed for a while as I learned to bring the images into focus.

Take a moment to think about all the ways that you have noticed spirits or intuited things, meaning the times you didn't know how you knew something but you just knew it. How did you receive the information? Did you see it, hear it, feel it, or something else? How you perceived that information might be the main way that you will end up doing readings. At the same time, once you open up, you might find that you have other gifts you never knew you had.

Let's revisit the budding medium I spoke of earlier who sees words being typed in front of her. The minute we met, her gifts that she'd always known were there just started to open up. It is often said that when the student is ready, the teacher appears. Apparently, my deceased family had offered to help her develop her skills. I never thought my family was that interesting until I heard her, as another medium, describe my deceased grandfather as being like Joe Pesci. He didn't really look or act like Joe Pesci, but to someone unfamiliar with New York or the East Coast, I could see how my very New York grandfather would be perceived and connected to as being like Joe Pesci since that was someone she was familiar with and could connect to.

During the course of the same reading, this budding medium started to ask me about another spirit she kept seeing. She described this person in detail, starting with the hair. She started with that feature because she, the medium, is a hairstylist and her go-to thing is doing hair.

The budding medium went on with the reading by describing mannerisms, occupation, and information about the spirit. I could not validate any of the information that was coming through, although I suspected that it was a deceased relative of mine that I did not know very well. I asked her to feel like what the deceased person's relationship was to me, and she said the person was a great aunt. I also told her to ask other questions to help us validate who the deceased person was, such as how she died.

The first thing that is important once you link with a spirit is to ascertain who the spirit is. That doesn't mean finding a name; it means finding a relationship. You need to discover the spirit's relationship to the client that you are doing the reading for.

You may ask, "But, Lisa, HOW do I make a link?"

You were born to do this. You've been doing it all your life. Just relax and stop trying to control the way the information comes to you. That's when the spirit usually comes in.

During a demonstration of mediumship (aka platform or gallery style mediumship), I may await my turn to read and not know who my spirit is. Right before I get up to demonstrate, though, it usually comes to me. Once that happens, I have no choice but to say what I'm getting, whether it is the pictures in my mind or the feelings that I have around me. When the time comes for you to link with Spirit, it will happen, just as this happens to me. You will also find that the way you link or who you can link with may vary as you become more and more experienced. Even though I have been doing readings for many years now, I can still be surprised at how things come through.

One day a woman came to me for a half-hour reading at a psychic fair I was doing. She told me she wanted to work with the other side for the readings. I asked who she'd like me to try to connect with, and she gave me the name "Ramses." My first thought was that I hoped it was not the Egyptian god Ramses. To confirm that it was not the Egyptian god, I asked her if Ramses was someone she knew in this life, to which she said yes. This helped me establish my link with Ramses.

I began by verifying details: he was muscular, and he had something specific about his hair or what he did to his hair. I then told her I couldn't quite make out what he looked like. She said, "He was a dog."

As I have mentioned before, I often connect with a client through pets. I'm not, however, ordinarily a pet medium. Normally, when I see a pet come through with a deceased person it's usually a dog, but I only see a picture of the dog with the client. This dog, however, was talking to me. As the reading progressed, I didn't overthink things and simply continued.

I told her everything the dog said about his life, his illness, and his relationship with her, and it truly touched her. All the while, in the back of my mind, I was thinking, "I don't do pets. How did this happen?" Suddenly, it hit me. I asked her if Ramses must have been a dog that thought he was human, and she laughed. I had been completely befuddled, but at that moment, it made sense to me. I told her that he must have had a very loving, powerful connection with her to come through that day because I normally only link with deceased people. She agreed about that connection.

Even though I didn't understand how I was doing that reading when it started, by the end, the connection was very clear to me. As you continue along your journey, you will find that how you connect with Spirit may evolve, just as your gift itself will evolve.

The Different Types of Evidence

Evidence is the part of a medium reading that gives you specific details about the person or situation you are bringing through for your client. Evidence gives your client the details that a stranger would not know, or not many other people would know. This can come through as factual evidence or emotional evidence, depending on the information that you receive.

Factual Evidence

Solid evidence goes deeper than the surface. For example, you might tell a client, "I'm feeling like I have a grandmother here. I see her in an apron and feel like she liked to bake." That may be a start to evidence, but it is not good evidence unless the grandmother in question actually had that about her personality. You can start with something general, but you need to find specifics to validate who it is you are linking to during the reading.

Further evidence could be obtained by asking that grandmother that is coming through what she wants to give you or by asking her what she wants to show you. She might show you a memory box, and if you ask her to open it for you, that might show you pieces of her life. She might show you that she had to go to work during a hard time for the family, or even during a war. She might show you a sickness that someone in her family had. You will never know what information the spirit you're bringing through might give to you unless you take the chance to translate what that spirit is giving you and bring it through to the client.

You may start to develop symbols that come through during a reading that will help you provide evidence. For instance, when I see a flag that is folded during a reading, I associate that with a military connection. When I see a headstone, I associate that as spirits acknowledging where they are buried or something special about the headstone. As I have developed, I have learned how to go deeper and ask the spirit to show me what's on the headstone.

Sometimes you will be connecting with a spirit that shows you a photograph, perhaps even a wall with photos on it or pictures in a photo album. Seeing that image symbolizes for me that the client was likely either just looking at photographs of the spirit or has a wall dedicated to the memory of that lost loved one at home. By taking that image further and trying to see what the picture is of, I can provide further evidence for the client. As you develop, you can try to do the same thing.

If you think you should be getting names and are not, do not worry. Many mediums do not get names. I rarely get names, but I do from time to time when it is important to the reading. To me it is natural not to always receive a name. In fact, one of my teachers once say that when she comes through during a reading after she's crossed to the other side, she's not going to say, "Hi. This is Mavis". Doing so would be unnatural to her, and it very well may the same for other spirits as well.

If there are ways that you are looking for evidence and have a hard time finding it, think of the way that you typically like to receive or communicate information in life. Is it on a computer screen? If it is, then imagine that you are seeing evidence on the computer screen in your mind. That might make it easier for you to bring through the factual evidence that would help your client know who it is you are communicating with during a reading.

I had one reading recently where I was seeing what looked like a painting to me or some sort of very nice portrait of the client's mother. Based on a series of images I was getting as evidence, she revealed that her mother had once had a picture taken by a very famous photographer. It turned out that what I had been seeing was an oil painting

I had of my great-grandmother. The picture had been famous at the time and had once been in a museum. Perhaps, had I gone deeper I could have gotten that it meant her mother had worked with a famous artist of some sort. The next time that portrait comes into my head, I will realize that it means more than the portrait of my grandmother and think about the details associated with it. I now know that there's more than meets the eye to the images I see during a reading, and I strive to go deeper to help produce the correct evidence for my client that her loved one is trying to bring through.

Emotional Evidence

There is also emotional evidence. This kind of evidence doesn't really bring through hard facts but may bring through a message that your client really needs. It may be that your client needs to hear an apology or to know someone who has passed has some other important message beyond a simple "I love you." Those things are emotional evidence. For example, I had a reading during which the client's sister came through and had to take responsibility for her death and apologize to the client for all the times she'd broken promises to the client. That's emotional evidence because it gave my client closure that hard facts could not have done.

Important Things to Remember About Medium Readings

When you do readings, you are still human. Part of our humanity may want something such as not to invade the client's privacy. I once did a reading for someone whose privacy I wasn't sure if I wanted to invade, partly because I was a little afraid that I'd be wrong because what I was going to say was so specific that it would be a clear "yes" or "no" answer. Because of that fear, I skirted around the issue. I simply revealed that the client was in a relationship that was having some problems, that the two had been together a long time, and that the client was wondering if they both wanted the same things or if it was time for a change. That's about as deep as I got. My client, who happened to be one of my teachers, gave me feedback that I was right on the surface, but it would have meant more if I had been able to reveal more. In other words, if I had taken that chance and gone deeper to reveal the information I really was getting but didn't say during the reading, then the client would have benefited more from the reading

In readings, remember the client gets what he or she needs, not what he or she wants to hear. Many psychic mediums do both medium readings and psychic readings in their practice. I have heard of some that do one or the other, but I do both. You can choose whether you want to ask your client what they want to know or to just let the information flow. If you trust what you are getting and reveal it, the client will always get what he or she needs but not always what he or she wants.

Another important thing to remember is that no medium is 100 percent correct. Sprit needs to come alive through us and our mediumship. That's what is the most important. You must feel the true joy and peace of what you are doing to really continue with this work. It's natural to be nervous, but even if you dread a reading because of stage fright or fear that you will be wrong, remember that once you step into the true power and blend with a spirit's soul you will forget that dread or nervousness. You were chosen to do this work because you CAN. Remember that.

For the most part, as your medium work evolves, you will not have to ask a specific question; Spirit will give you the answers. That's when you become the detective. If Spirit shows you a framed picture, try to go deeper and see what's in the frame to give more evidence to the client. Remember: it's Spirit giving you the answers, even if you think what is coming through makes no sense or feels a bit nuts.

I was giving a woman a reading about her brother who had passed. I saw a photo in a frame which showed the two of them laughing on a roller coaster. If I would have let myself get in the way and discarded that image for fear I was inventing it, she never would have been able to reveal she had a photo like that of her and her brother. As the reading went on, I started to feel pain in my ankle that impacted my walking. Through my own pain and limping, I was able to bring through his likeness because he had limped. Spirit used me to be able to connect with his essence soul-to-soul to bring that piece of evidence through.

Sometimes the evidence is right in front of you, but because it's so obvious to you, you discard it. That may mean your client is missing out on something because you were afraid of the word "no."

Things That May Cause a "No" From Your Client

There are several things that may happen during a reading that cause you to receive a "no" from your client.

- Incorrect relationship
- Overstating the message
- Wrong recipient
- Wrong choice of words or translation
- A nervous client

Incorrect Relationship

When you reveal the incorrect relationship of the spirit who is communicating through you to the client, you might say you have a father when it's really a grandfather or someone like a father. Another possibility if that the grandfather is not who the client wants to speak to, so the client doesn't recognize it really is his or her grandfather. While the client might tell you that the information is incorrect, you can often use that information to help you dig deeper and find the correct connection.

Overstating the Message

There are also times where you could bring through a grandfather but overstate the message by saying, "You were very close to him," when, in fact, the client was not because maybe the grandfather had died before the client was born. You may assume that they were close because most people are close to their grandparents, but that is not always the case. That word choice can result in the client not recognizing his or her grandfather at all because they were never close.

I once did a reading where I was seeing someone patriotic. To me, that meant an American flag since I am American. I then launched into many things I was seeing about the country I was from. However, the client I was reading for was from the United Kingdom. Because I overstated the details of the country I was from, my client did not recognize the deceased. In this case, the person coming through for my client was British, and the person's way of being patriotic was by being fascinated by and loyal to the British monarchy. By simply stating, "Do you understand that the person coming through was patriotic?" instead, I could have not lost the client by telling him too much right away.

In a public reading, you might also overstate the message by saying something like: "I have a father with me that was in the US Navy, and I see him on a ship which, to me, means his career was in service to his country." A message like that might have no one raise their hand. Instead, you could simply say, "I have a father, or step-father, who passed that had a connection to military service." You then keep it a bit more general but don't lose half the audience by overstating who the person is. This allows more of a chance for a connection with several people. You can build the evidence to find the right recipient from there, by saying, "I also feel he died of a heart attack or something related to his heart." If you take it piece by piece, it's easier not to overstate the message.

Wrong Recipient

During a demonstration, group reading, or sitting with more than one person in the room, you may have the right dead person but the wrong person in the room. In a group or large demonstration, if you do not change to the correct recipient, this can cause a switch, which is when one spirit stops communicating because the medium is speaking to the wrong person. You may have a woman's father coming through, but since you're talking to a man on the other side of the room, the father's spirit may back up and let a spirit whose recipient is the man step in.

I was in a class where the students were doing demonstrations, and this happened. The medium got up and said that she was communicating with a father or grandfather that was in a marching band. My grandfather was in a band, but not a marching band. Still, out of ten people in the room, no one could identify with the information given, so finally I raised my hand. We learned later that at that point a switch occurred between two spirits. I wasn't the recipient for the first spirit, so when I was the only one who claimed him, my relative stepped in. Even though I was not the actual recipient for the first spirit, it ended up being a very meaningful reading for me. Later when the class was discussing the readings, we learned that someone else had missed the reference to a marching band during the reading because it wasn't stated exactly as they'd remembered the band being.

I could tell during the reading in which the switch occurred that the medium didn't really think the message was for me. When the switch occurred, however, and I realized it was then my grandfather, I took the message with great enthusiasm, so she stayed with me. There are times when you might have to stay true to the direction you think you should be going in or to the person you are with. As you continue to do this work and practice, you will get better at doing that and more confident in doing so.

Wrong Word Choice or Translation

Sometimes during a reading, you may make the wrong choice of words or translation. In the example above when I was the wrong recipient for the reading, the medium used the words "marching band" and the correct recipient didn't understand the meaning. That doesn't mean that calling it a marching band was wrong, but sometimes the recipient may need a little more.

There are also times where the best thing to do is to keep it simple if you are not sure. "How do you connect to the color purple?" or "I'm seeing a purple article of clothing," might be better than saying, "Do you have a purple shirt of your mother's?" The last option gives the client the opportunity to say "no" because it really was a purple dress and not a shirt.

Nervous Client

Let's be honest, there are more times than not when we may have a nervous client. This can happen in a live audience reading because the recipient may not recognize that the evidence provided by the medium is really for him or her or may be afraid to raise his or her hand. There are times when you will bring forth someone that has passed that your client didn't expect to hear from. The recipient may not recognize the person either due to nerves or because the evidence coming through just wasn't at the forefront of his or her mind. It could also be that the recipient has never had a reading before and doesn't know what to expect or how to react.

I was recently read by someone else in a private sitting, and one of my childhood friends came through. It took me forever to recognize my childhood friend because I was just not expecting her to come through.

As a psychic medium, I might forget that my client can be nervous because I connect with the other side much more than he or she does. If this is a person's first time—or seventh time—seeing to a psychic medium, nerves can be a factor.

Remember that no matter the reason for your client saying "no," Spirit does not fail us. They want us to connect to their loved ones more than we do. If at first, we don't get the message correct or it doesn't connect with our client, they will work with us to try to get the right message to the person they love. More times than not, that happens even if we get a few negative responses right away.

The Story

Readings evolve from our experiences. Sometimes the information you receive, regardless of how you receive the information, mirrors or resembles your own experiences. I was in a class with other mediums in which the teacher asked us information about his grandfather. The first thing that I felt was that the grandfather was hitting on me. I had never experienced that from someone on the other side, but I blurted out, "I think he was a lady's man."

I knew that it was risky for me to say that about my teacher's grandfather, but my teacher encouraged me to go on. I did, and a story evolved. The teacher said later that no one else had gotten that depth of information about his grandfather, but I believe the reason I got it was that I had similar experiences in my own life with a deceased male family member.

There are some mediums I have heard that are rock stars with evidence. They may simply state names, numbers, dates, and relationships in short statements and move on. But your loved one was a person and had a life, didn't they? The same is true with your client's loved one, and you need to take the time to let their story develop.

Once I brought through a spirit that had an accent very different than mine but that I could imitate pretty well. Using that accent ended up connecting the recipient to who it was communicating through me and to the fact that the message was for her. Not only was that evidence, that accent was part of the story of her life, too.

When we talk about things like making a link and perhaps taking on the likeness of someone, that's part of their story. When we talk about the way they felt in life, that's part of their story.

If you can rock the factual evidence, that's great. Just try to remember that every person you are bringing through had a life and with that life came a story, not just facts.

CHAPTER 5 – PUBLIC DEMONSTRATIONS

Demonstrations (Live Audience Readings)

Public demonstrations, also known as live audience or gallery readings, are reading for a group of people that can range from five to over 100. As part of a Spiritualist church service, mediums give public demonstrations during the service. Other public demonstrations may occur at psychic expos, metaphysical fairs, or fee-for-service events that mediums set up. You may not choose to do demonstrations as part of your practice, but I have found that public demonstration work has found me, and I do it as part of my work.

A good practice when on stage is to take a glass of water with you. You can sip on it when you have a pause in information or between links if you are doing more than one reading. On stage, you are also working with the element of time, so public demonstrations are not the best place to practice your techniques. You need to do that during your private sittings. Public demonstrations may be scary at first, but once you stand in the power of Spirit, you should be able to deliver messages to the recipients they are intended for.

You do not have to have a background on stage, only the desire to serve Spirit. When I do demonstrations, I usually do not have a contact (spirit) until right before I stand up or go on stage. As a general rule, if you have what you feel is a contact that has been with you all day, it's not good to take that contact with you on stage. This is because you usually have the most powerful link with Spirit at the time you receive the information. If you have had the contact for hours, the most powerful piece of the information you were meant to receive may already be gone.

Recently, I was at an expo doing readings all day. I had stopped after doing about six hours of readings, and I was scheduled to be one of five mediums to do an hour-long audience reading. Each medium would work about ten to fifteen minutes. When I told the organizer that I had stopped doing readings earlier from exhaustion, she asked if I was sure I wanted to continue. I looked at her and confidently said, "Spirit does not disappoint." She laughed and said that she says the same thing.

All five of the mediums at that event had a totally different style, so keep in mind that your style may not be exactly like mine. It was my first time in that geographical area, so I presumed the people didn't know me. As such, I started out by explaining who I was, how long I had been practicing, and what my plan was for the demonstration. I explained that while I am a psychic and medium, I was there to read their dead people. I also explained that they could help me in two ways. First, they could own their dead people. When you do a live audience reading, it's sometimes hard for people to raise their hands at the idea that the person coming through might be their person. By asking them to own their dead people, it encouraged them to take this leap of faith. Second, they needed to think outside of the box. While a person might be there to hear from their mom or dad, with Spirit directing the flow, it could be someone else, and the audience needed to be prepared for that.

My first audience reading was a father who had passed away, and he was so specific in his evidence that he was claimed rather easily by his daughter. My next audience reading was also rather specific in style. I was getting an eccentric aunt, or great-aunt, who had a prominent role in the recipient's life. She was meticulous about the way she dressed and looked, and she seemed as though she thought the world was a stage. When I started talking, I had two hands go up, but the more I continued with what she was telling me, it was clear which person the aunt was there for.

With the aunt, she kept showing me a piano. I asked one of the potential recipients about the piano, but she did not play, nor did the aunt. I explained that the aunt continued to show me a piano. Finally, that potential recipient realized that her sister, who was sitting next to her at the time, played the piano. We all laughed when the connection was figured out. This example is important because it illustrates how hard it can be for an audience member to claim evidence or for you to relay it in a way that the audience member can claim it. Had the woman not realized that about her sister, I probably would have left the piano for then and kept going, trusting that if the piano was supposed to come back, it would.

In a live demonstration, you need to do your best to find your recipient. If you say something like, "I have a mother with breast cancer," that is usually not specific enough to narrow it down to one recipient. As such, you will have to work with the numerous hands that go up to see who the message is for. You should be more successful if you give a more specific message, such as, "The person worked making and repairing watches." Something that specific is likely to cause a fewer number of hands go up.

Also, when you stand up to give the initial message, less is more. Give only a few pieces of evidence, as it should not take you more than four or five pieces to find your recipient. I learned from one of my teachers that I used to have a habit of giving too much evidence right away. He called it "verbal diarrhea." When you say too much, you run the risk of losing someone that may be the correct recipient because you gave too much detail and the person feels uncomfortable raising his or her hand.

When looking for the recipient, you should let Spirit guide you. You can attempt to find your recipient by either being direct and asking a specific person you feel led to if he or she can answer a specific question related to the evidence you've brought through or by saying that you feel led to a certain area of the crowd and asking if anyone in that direction recognizes the information coming through. If no one raises a hand, then you can throw it out to the general audience to see if anyone can identify with the evidence you've brought through.

The Switch

When working a crowd, you need to be careful to is find the right recipient. As I mentioned in the last chapter, when you try to connect the spirit coming through with the incorrect recipient, that spirit may step back and let the spirit for that recipient come through. When this happens, it is called a switch. For example, if a medium is bringing through information from a father but connects it to the wrong child, the father may step back and allow that child's father to come through.

When there is a switch, it may not be your fault. It is just important that you go with your gut. I was at a recent demonstration where there were two people nodding and saying "yes" for several minutes into the reading. The next day, many of the mediums present for that demonstration were still wondering whose reading it was really supposed to be. I believe there was a switch partway through the reading because of a subtle difference in the first part and second part of the reading that related to the mention of a specific piece of evidence, a bowl of fruit. I believe that the first lady receiving the reading from her loved one got the message she was supposed to receive during the first part of the reading, and then the spirit switched and the second person received her message from second part of the reading.

CHAPTER 6: TOUGH CLIENTS – TOUGH READINGS

Readings sometimes do not turn out like expected, either for you as the reader or the client as the recipient. In this chapter, I will share with you some of the experiences from my own journey when this has happened, both as a client and as the psychic medium doing the reading. These experiences can be difficult to work through. You will also find in your practice that there are other ways in which readings, and clients, can be tough. We'll discuss a few of those here, too.

As a general rule, I do not read for family or friends that I know really well. To me, I can't be objective with them, and my knowledge of their lives already defeats the purpose of an authentic reading. I have made exceptions to this rule very little, and when I have, it has not always been an easy thing to do.

I once did a reading for someone I knew but only at a very superficial level: she had been a student in some of my classes. Many people I read for have talents of their own, either as a psychic, a medium, or both, and she was one of them. As we started the reading, she said she wanted to contact her sister, and she also wanted to tell me how her sister had died. I stopped her and asked her to let her sister do the work and bring through evidence so that we would know it was really her sister coming through.

I began by saying, "I see her clutching her chest and feel that she died of a heart attack."

I could sense hesitation from my client, so I asked her to give me a "yes" or "no" answer. The client responded, "Sort of."

I said, politely, that I was not trying to be hard on her as a client, but that we should limit it to "yes" or "no" answers. I assured her that she could tell me things later if she wanted to fill in the details.

As the reading continued, I could tell that some of the things I was saying fit, but she wasn't validating them for me. I realized that she probably had a certain way in mind that she thought her sister should come through or be answering. I said, "Remember, we don't choose the information they give to us, and it's not always what we'd expect them to say or do." After that, the reading flowed a bit better.

As the reading went on, the client told me she knew her sister had a hiding place in their house, but she didn't know where it was. I started to see a picture of an old house with a trick floor board that came up. I relayed this information to my client. At first, she couldn't figure out what I meant, so I started describing the house. I asked if it was an old house, and she said that it was. I then proceeded to describe every detail of what I was seeing, down to the location of the room where the floor board was. Along the way, I'd check to see if what I was seeing was correct, and the client verified it was. I told her the exact area where I saw it, and it wasn't the answer either one of us were expecting. Rather than get in my own way when she didn't understand what I was talking about, I worked with Spirit to describe it in a way we could both understand.

As a client, I have also experienced times when I came into a reading with my own expectations. It took 14 years for my grandfather to start coming through from the other side. When he finally did, I was in a class where I was getting lots of mini-readings from other students. We would trade roles as the reader and the "client." I had my own ideas of what I thought my grandfather would say, thinking he would bring through something I readily remembered he liked or something about our relationship. Instead, every single person that brought him through that day mentioned his wood saw, which I had forgotten all about. My grandfather had a table saw in the basement that he loved; he would run it early in the morning and not care if he woke the whole house up. It was not what I had expected to come through, but that was evidence to me that it was actually him, especially when medium after medium that never knew my grandfather brought the same piece of evidence through.

As the reader, I also have expectations for the readings I provide. I give almost as many psychic readings as I do medium readings, and, as I mentioned before, one very difficult question for me to hear is: "Is my husband cheating?" The first time I gave a reading where the answer to that question was "yes," the client and I both finished the reading in tears. As a result, for a long time, I refused to answer that question. In fact, I'd usually tell my guides not to bring me clients that had that question. For a few years, it worked, but eventually the subject came up again when an acquaintance asked for an emergency reading because her husband had asked for a divorce out of the blue. I felt that I didn't know her well enough to know the details and allow my own thoughts to get in the way, so I did the reading for her.

The reading was very clear to me, and it was filled with difficult messages for the client. I even apologized and said I hoped I was wrong. Of course, I was not wrong because it wasn't me giving the message: it was being channeled through me. I finished the reading crying hard, just like I had in the first reading with such a question. I asked my guides, "Why me? Why do I have to be the one that delivers messages like this?"

They clearly replied, "Lisa, because you CAN."

Not everyone can give the message that contains hard truths, but it was something that I had been chosen to do. I used to want all my clients to leave my sessions happy. For the most part, they do. But, sometimes they aren't coming to me to find happiness; they are there to find truth. I've learned now that clients always get what they need, and that's not necessarily what they want. It's hard for me not to get in my own way and wonder if the information is correct. Now when I have a tough message to deliver, I just think to myself that my guides once told me that I deliver the truth because I can.

In one particular reading, I received information about the client's son, or what I believed to be her son. When I felt his energy, I was getting that this was an emotionally troubled young man. I saw the number 17, so I thought he was 17. She told me that he was 29. I continued and said that I felt like there was a medical problem with him that was not life threatening but had something to do with his dark emotional state. I also mentioned that it felt like he might even be suicidal.

All the information was coming to me so clearly and quickly, I had to give it like I was receiving it. I imagine the word "suicidal" would scare anyone to hear about their child, and by reviewing the evidence that came up in reading, we ascertained that a medical condition he had when he was 17 had depressed him, and he had been suicidal at that time. At the end of the reading, I again reassured her that the information that had come through had been about the past and that he was not suicidal at the time. Still, it could not have been an easy message to hear because it was not an easy one to relay.

We, as in the people that give readings, can sometimes also be the worst clients, so to speak. Recently, I did a reading for someone that also did readings. When I connected with her father, I felt water. She verified that and then told me she was seeing something similar, which told me she was tuning in, too. She'd done that a couple of times in the reading already, and I finally stopped and said, "Excuse me. I'm doing the reading." That's not easy to have to do, but sometimes when reading a peer or student, you have to do that.

In 2015, I went to Arthur Findlay College in the United Kingdom for the first time. I'd heard about it from both a trusted teacher and peers, and I know that I heard about it when I was ready to go. I'd signed up for the class a year in advance, and right before I went, I knew I was supposed to go because I had started to feel like a rather lazy medium. Perhaps, I was being self-critical, but, perhaps, I also knew I could challenge myself to do better. It's not all mothers and grandmothers that have passed, and I wanted to challenge myself to do better in both private sittings and on stage, especially since I had not had much experience on stage doing live demonstrations at the time.

Right before going to the class, around the time I had begun to think that it was a good thing I was doing the class because I felt lazy, I did a large psychic expo. It was a two-day all-day local event at which I did many readings back-to-back. The first women I did a reading for wanted to bring her ex-husband through, so I started to tell her what I was getting. She seemed to get more and more frustrated with each piece of evidence I tried to present. She ended up telling me that she remembered a specific time that he was sitting on the bed and left his imprint on the bed. It was at that point that I gave her back half of her money and told her that she'd probably do better at someone else's booth for the reading because we weren't connecting. In a way, she wouldn't let me connect because she had in her head such a clear idea of what SHE wanted that she wasn't listening to anything Spirit had to tell her.

Another one that came to me was one of my peers at the expo. While it seemed like it would be an honor to do a reading for a peer, she was also a very tough client because she didn't seem to like anything I had to say when I linked with her father. She kept tuning in to make sure I was right. As I mentioned earlier, this is not something that you can allow as a reader because it if you that is doing the reading and not vice versa. As a former teacher told me, people aren't paying you to hear themselves talk.

As with any business, you are going to encounter both tough readings and tough clients. It's your job to set some boundaries with your readings. It will not be the same for every person, but don't be afraid to tell your clients to please let go of any expectations they may have for what they will get during the reading so that they can accept a reality that very well may differ from that.

I recently did a reading for someone that I could tell was intuitive in a very powerful way. She told me about a spirit that was attached to her and about another psychic she had visited. She wanted to find out what I saw as a second opinion, so to speak. I started out by telling her that generally I don't believe in spirit attachments.

At first in the reading, I saw the word "Prince," as in the musician that passed away. I decided to continue because the client had noted she had a celebrity in mind, and, just like anyone would, I didn't want to get it wrong. The fact that she seemed so determined to have a name for the spirit and had told me that she had already visited another psychic almost seemed to intimidate me. When the reader—me or you—gets nervous, that can throw the whole reading off.

As I did the reading, it seemed I kept hitting dead ends or kept going the wrong direction. I could tell that she put a mental wall up when she didn't get what she wanted from me, so I asked my angels for help. I then started to focus on other parts of her life, and the reading started to go better. The whole time I was talking about the other parts of her life, I kept seeing the word "Prince" in all forms. Finally, I said, "What's your connection to Prince?" That was what she had wanted to hear the whole reading.

I know I'm growing as I do this work because, not so long ago, I would have just given her a partial refund and thought it was me (and berated myself afterwards). I realize now it was both of us: it was an exchange of energy. Sometimes in personal interactions, one person or the other, or both parties, can get defensive or start off on the wrong foot, so to speak. Sometimes you work through it; sometimes you don't. The more I grow and realize these people are coming to me for a reason, to the more I am able to work through it and not give up.

In your practice, I encourage you to work through your fears at least once or twice before you give a person a refund or feel like you gave a poor reading and berate yourself afterwards. As with anything, being a reader, whether as a psychic or as a medium, is a gift and a talent. You must build and grow that talent, just like any other talent, and trying to work through your fear in a live reading will certainly help you do that.

Sometimes when a reading seems tough, it's because the client doesn't really want the reading or the client is not really open to what is coming through. You will not always have everything validated for you in the way you hope. Some clients are very stoic, and you may think you failed them when, in fact, it's the opposite. Others may just simply not be open to having a reading, and you may have to simply end the reading because you cannot read for someone who is not open to it.

A woman came to me at a psychic expo after two of her friends had recommended me because of the readings I had given them earlier in the day. She told me she'd never had a reading but had come since her friends had urged her to do so. We did a general reading, and in the reading, it came up that she was an empty-nester and was wondering what was next in her life. Near the end of the reading, I asked her for confirmation for a piece of evidence, and she launched into a speech about how she had never advertised during her career and did not agree with the glitz and glamour of advertising or the fame aspect of the business, implying that I did. She then told me that all I had given her so far was general information. She said that anyone could get the stuff I had about her being an empty-nester and that I had not told her anything specific.

I was taken aback, but I asked her what she wanted to do about the five remaining minutes of the reading. She said she wanted me to go on, but she was clearly still impatient with the reading. I stopped and said, "I'm sorry, but I'm done."

She said, "No, we have a few minutes. You can still try.".

I replied, "No, I'm done with this reading. You have shown disrespect to both my business and me, and I will not charge you for this, but the reading is done."

I wasn't mad at her, and she shook my hand and thanked me in the end (probably for not charging her). If she had told her friends she didn't want a reading, they probably should have listened to her because, as I mentioned before, you can't really read for someone that doesn't want a reading.

I recently tried to do a reading for a woman that had lost a child. After several tries, the only evidence I received was that the child died in an accident. It was near the end of a day in which I had done many readings, and I wondered if it was me and I'd hit the wall, so to speak. By that, I mean that I had done so many readings I was no longer able to do them. The woman then told me that another medium had the same experience when her sister had tried to have him brought through. She revealed that the child had not been gone that long, and I offered to keep going to see if her other deceased family could give more insight. She chose not to continue, so I did not charge her.

One of my teachers told me that he once had a client come to him, and he, as the reader, couldn't make a link. My teacher felt bad about this because the man had driven so far for the reading. While the client was preparing to leave, my teacher asked the client if the he and his son had not spoken when the son was alive. The client verified that. It was entirely possible that the son didn't want to talk to the father from the other side, either.

There will be tough readings and tough clients. It's part of the business. No two clients are alike, and no two situations are alike. They all receive information differently and have different needs. We have to try to be patient with it, work around it, and have integrity when a connection is not made, which may mean not charging our clients. While you may choose not to do that, I do it at times simply because it's my brand and reputation.

CHAPTER 7: STAYING DRIVEN - OVERCOMING THE LAZY MEDIUM AND AVOIDING PSYCHIC SCAMMERS

The Lazy Medium

We all have times as psychic mediums when we do not feel motivated, whether it is during a reading or towards our profession in general. We do not try as hard as we can, and we act like what I call "the lazy medium," or the medium who is burned out or too frustrated to try harder. This often leads to focusing more on the esoteric side of things or being too general because we don't want to push as hard as we can to find the real message. Even though we all feel like this from time to time, we can push through it and get back to being productive and genuine in our readings.

The first time I started feeling like a lazy medium when I gave readings, I decided it was time to go to another psychic development class. I felt like the same information was coming through again and again, which is not a good thing because every client is different. I couldn't help wondering if I could be doing something more. Could I be going deeper? To find out, I had to challenge myself and work on developing my skills.

What I want for each of you is for you to challenge yourself, as well. As I mentioned earlier in the book, it's time to take it easy on the fluffy unicorn and rainbow messages. You'll do better for yourself and your clients if you strive to be the best psychic medium you can be. Even if it is a "sunshine and rainbows" reading that the client wants, that may not be what he or she needs.

Another time I find myself feeling lazy in readings, in retrospect, is when I get nervous. This may happen to you if you have a client that either doesn't believe you or doesn't want to hear the message that you are bringing through. When this happens, you react as anyone in that situation would and become intimidated and nervous. This can, undoubtedly, disrupt a reading. As psychic mediums, we are the channel for Spirit, and when we get nervous, our energy blocks that channel. At the same time, it is easy to get discouraged and not keep trying when we feel like someone is not going to listen, no matter how hard we try.

I once gave a reading where I felt intimidated by the client when she wasn't getting the information she wanted. I could feel it both in her body language and energy. Suddenly, I felt insecure and nervous. I almost told her that it was not working and gave her money back. That, however, wasn't fair to either of us: the woman had driven a long way to see me for a scheduled appointment. Instead of giving in to the urge to be a lazy medium, I decided to ask my angels and guides for help.

I changed the subject from the one we'd been discussing where she had given me so many negative responses and had seemed like she was not getting what she wanted. I started to talk about her life at home with her family, which she validated for me. I could still tell she wanted more, but going to a different place allowed me to get out of that moment of fear and move forward. Eventually, we got the information she'd wanted to hear because once I was clearer and in the power of Spirit, exactly what she needed—and wanted—to hear about came up.

One lazy medium habit that bothers me when I'm the recipient of a reading is when I ask a real question and get an explanation having to do with the esoteric meaning of the energy around me rather than the real life answer I'm seeking. I recently received a reading and asked about one of my cats. Instead of answering my question, I was told I was bringing dark energy home from work. Not only was I unsure what the medium meant by that or was even referring to, it was vague and did not come close to answering the question I asked. I, too, could keep my career going by just staying relatively general in readings, but that would not serve me or my clients. If we want to be better at this, then we have to challenge ourselves to keep providing evidence and being specific when giving a reading.

Working as a psychic medium, I enjoy the opportunity to sometimes watch my peers work. It's always interesting to me because we're all so different. I recently was at a demonstration of three different mediums and found that two of them had very good readings but were strangely similar in format. It reinforced to me that even experienced mediums can become lazy and limit themselves to solely bringing through easy spirits to work with or to talking about one specific piece of evidence in each reading.

I once heard of a medium who called herself "The Grandma Medium" because she only brought through grandmothers. By affirming that time and again, she only got grandmothers. Sometimes we must open our mind to other possibilities. Sometimes we must stretch ourselves and want more. That might mean it's time for another teacher, or it might mean it's time to let go and try something new in your readings.

I have decided that if this is my gift, then I want to use that to help others. In doing so, I believe it's my responsibility to be the best I can be, and hopefully you do, too. This is a lifetime of service and also a career, and I am always a student striving for more.

Depending on your experience level, when you begin to feel the possibility of becoming a lazy medium, you may want to take more classes. You may want to take lots of them at first, but even when you are in your own practice, it's still good to refresh or renew your skills by taking a class every couple of years. You will continue to learn something new to develop your existing practice.

Psychic Scammers

There are people out there in every business that are dishonest. In this field, there are scammers just like in every other field. There are the ones that say you have a curse or an attachment and want to charge $5,000 to remove it. Perhaps, they want to help you find your true love but talk you into spending thousands of dollars on readings, buying products, or buying them things. Unfortunately, psychic scammers are out there, and they are a discredit to those of us who work diligently in our field to help others.

There are things that upset all of us, and one thing that upsets me in a reading is when clients tell me that another psychic has told them that they have an attachment that may be evil or not good for them. I have no problem telling them I don't believe that and that I think that is not good information for them to have been told or believe. Too many psychics use that type of information to mislead clients into spending money that doesn't need to be spent, in my opinion.

Although I am a psychic medium, I have worked in finance my whole life, especially with the stock market. I have seen more than one of my psychic peers make a prediction that the stock market is going to crash. This upsets me because it's ignorant and is a way to scare and scam people, whether or not it's intentional. The stock market ebbs and flows, and there are many more rules and regulations that have been created to prevent anything like the early stock market crash from happening again. The stock market is typically for long term investors because of its natural ebb and flow. The market has been doing very well for the last few years (called a bull market), so it is very likely going to go down at some point in the near future since that is its natural cycle. The only thing anyone should worry about is making investments that are too aggressive for their tolerance level.

As of the time of writing this book, this type of prediction has been the fad prediction, in my opinion. Whether the prediction is right or wrong, I personally don't support psychic mediums predicting disaster as if they want toot their own horn like: "You heard it here first, folks". To me, that's not professional. Why would you want to build your brand by predicting disaster? I don't support a business that does it. To me, that's kind of like even when you know a potential client or the client's loved one is going to die, you don't say it. I'm in this business to help people, not make them miserable or make money based on scaring people. Even though people may need to hear difficult messages in readings, it is very different from broadcasting disaster to the public or giving a message that will only do harm.

CHAPTER 8: SELF-CARE AS A PSYCHIC MEDIUM

One thing I spoke a bit about in my first book, *Gifted*, was about boundaries and protection. It's important to do as you feel guided when it comes to that. My general practice is that I usually ask the angels for protection and leave it at that. I generally ask Archangel Michael, or St. Michael as some of you may know him. I just know I'm protected, and I usually ask for clients that will be for my greatest and highest good and vice versa. Some of you may have other prayers or things you do to prepare for a reading, and that is a personal decision for you, which is why it varies so from one person to the next.

Doing readings of any kind can be exhausting. Channeling Spirit is essentially using our bodies to bring through the information we receive for readings. One of my teachers stated that when you are reading, you are "the tube," meaning the information and energy flows through you as if you're a vessel or a tube. Sometimes when I do one reading for an hour, I feel tired. I recently did my first ever hour-long live audience reading. It never dawned on me, even with the amount of experience I have, how absolutely exhausting that would be.

When I do psychic fairs on weekends, I will do anywhere from 10 to 20 readings per day. They are mostly 15-minute readings, but some of them are 30-minute readings. Regardless, doing that many readings back-to-back can leave you exhausted. I sometimes do two-day events, and I'm really spent at the end of the second day. Once I am home or in my hotel room, I only do what's necessary (usually a meal) before crawling in bed for a long sleep.

One thing that I have learned over the course of doing many of these events is that I have to work time to for breaks and a lunch into my schedule, just like I would in any work day. The reason I am writing about this is that, even after all my years of practice with this, I still sometimes forget to do this if the day is busy and I don't have an assistant with me to make sure to write in those breaks for me.

If I'm doing a daylong expo with the hours of, say, 10 a.m. to 5 p.m., I usually start right away and then listen to my body for signs. Sometimes I may "hit the wall" earlier than 5 p.m., which means I'm too exhausted to do accurate readings, so I stop. I'd rather do that than risk my reputation by not giving the best reading I can when I'm too tired.

I've seen many of my peers at these events work straight through without eating or taking a break. There could be many reasons for them to do this that I do not know, but it can still have repercussions. I was recently at a festival where the woman sitting next to me did back-to-back readings all day. When I saw her the next day, she was exhausted, couldn't talk well, and had to have a healing before the event started. She told me that she was taking an hour lunch that day with no exceptions. She'd learned a lesson that I'm sure she'd known before but had forgotten in the name of helping others.

At one event, I had hit the wall at 3 p.m. with three hours to go in the work day. I'd traveled for that show, and it was difficult to have to turn people away that were asking for readings. Still even with time left to work and people needing help, I could not in good faith continue doing readings when I felt less than whole. In fact, I usually have to eat more than normal and be sure to stay hydrated. I had skipped meals and breaks that day, and afterwards I realized I may have lasted longer had I done so. I also have a sensitive stomach which is much more vulnerable when I do not take care of myself the way I should by taking breaks and eating right. That weekend, not only did I have to stop doing readings early, I had an awful stomachache the following night when it all caught up with me.

Over time, I have learned which events I do that are busy, and I usually ask an assistant to accompany me to those. Sometimes, when I do a new event and don't know whether I will need a helper or not, I find out the hard way, as you will, too. Those times are often the ones you can end up working all day with no down time. If you don't keep an eye on your own schedule and write in a lunch or the downtime that you need, you could suffer because of it.

The important thing to remember in all of this, no matter whether you do private sittings, fairs, or some other type of event, is to take care of YOU. Your body is your vehicle to do this work. It sounds so basic, but when you are in the energy of Spirit and helping people, it's easy to sometimes forget to take care of yourself.

Food Shaming

There seems to be a lot of talk in the enlightened community of what kind of food you should or should not eat or put into your body. I feel like a lot of people think that if they make eat a vegan diet, refrain from drinking alcohol, or refuse sweets that they will be a better clearer channel for Spirit. To me, this is a type of food shaming, and it does not really fit with my beliefs.

I remember one Thanksgiving (a big holiday where we all stuff ourselves silly with turkey and fixings in America), I saw a post from a prominent psychic about watching what we eat on this day because we must remember that we should be clear channels. I remember thinking to myself, "Why would we have to worry about that on Thanksgiving? We're not likely to be giving readings today."

One well-known person in the enlightened community often talks about how she's vegan and has given up alcohol, caffeine and more on her social media. One time, she made the statement that one of the people that she partnered with had really loved his occasional martinis, but that once he gave them up and became totally sober, then all his dreams came true. There is usually some small disclaimer to these posts that tells the reader to only give up what he or she feels guided to give up. My problem with this is that, as a follower of hers and a person who trusts her opinion, how could you not wonder or feel like you might be making a mistake if you continue to eat meat or indulge in one of the other items that she says you should give up?

I honestly don't think we came to Earth to sacrifice everything pleasurable just to give better readings. I eat fish, poultry, sugar, and wheat. I consume caffeine and drink a lot of diet soda. On occasion, I even drink alcohol or smoke a cigarette. Yes, some of it is known to be unhealthy, but to me, most everything in life seems to be unhealthy. We have to do some things that bring us pleasure, as long as we aren't overdoing it. There are also some who do overdo it from time to time and are still fine anyway.

None of the things I have just mentioned I consume have ever impacted my ability to be a psychic medium or do readings. We are still human and have to balance out the work we do in service to Spirit with our humanity.

My point is this: you do not have to be vegan or give up everything that is potentially bad for you in order to be a clear channel. To me, what makes us a clear or better channel—and, ultimately, better at giving readings—is practice.

Mercury Retrograde

The planet Mercury goes retrograde (moves backwards) four times a year, or once a quarter. The planet stays retrograde for about three weeks and has a snap at the beginning and the end for those sensitive to Mercury, which means you may feel it a bit before and after the official three weeks.

Some of the negative aspects of Mercury Retrograde, or MR as I like to refer to it, are that it's not a good time to sign contracts or buy electronics. At least, that's what a lot of people think. I believe it's fine if you do those things, as long as you know that you may need another Mercury Retrograde if you want to undo something you've done during that time. For example, you buy a home during MR then a few years later you put it on the market. It may seem like it takes a while to sell, but when you get to Mercury Retrograde, it suddenly sells. You needed another MR to undo what you did in a previous one.

I'm more superstitious about buying things like electronics *after* MR for fear that they were made during that time and were broken in some way. It still doesn't stop me from doing so, though. I can always return something if it doesn't work properly.

I am ultra-sensitive to MR because I have so many planets in my natal chart that are ruled by it. Perhaps because of that, there are times when I feel like we need an MR to right some wrongs, so to speak.

Mercury Retrograde is a great time to get things fixed. Think of anything that starts with "RE": repair, rejuvenate, and even relax. You may hear a truth you would not have otherwise heard in Mercury Retrograde.

I have a car that I knew would need new brakes in the next year or so. I had asked for them to be checked on more than one occasion, even though I didn't hear a squeal or feel some of the more typical signs of brakes going. I was still surprised that the mechanic never said that I needed new brakes since I was pretty sure I had the originals and my mileage was high enough to indicate they should have been changed by then. Then an MR came, and I just happened to take my car in for an oil change. The shop quickly called me back to say that the back brakes were so worn that I needed to change them as soon as possible. I was grateful they'd caught it because I had known something needed to be fixed and no one had ever caught it.

When I picked up the car later that day, they said I was really lucky because I'd been days away from driving with bare brakes, which would have damaged the car even more. That's the kind of truth that you learn in a beautiful way during Mercury Retrograde, even if it hurts at the time. It may even be something you may not have suspected or known about but comes to fruition anyway.

So, when you hear others that may say, "Beware, it's Mercury Retrograde," or complain about it, take it with a grain of salt. I think that we need things like this to cleanse and right some things that had been wrong before.

CHAPTER 9: PAST LIVES, SOUL GROUPS, AND PURPOSE

I saw a cute little Internet video of a baby that was lying next to his mother in bed and looking up at her like he was in love and so happy to be there. She just held her phone's camera up and seemed in awe of the fact that he seemed ecstatic to just be with her. I thought it was really lovely, and I also thought about past lives. Those two souls had been reunited and were together again: the little baby knew it, and that's why he and his mother were so connected.

There are those that may not connect with the concept of past lives. I didn't for a long time. But the more experience I get with doing readings and bringing souls through that want to speak to their loved ones, the more I realize it's true.

My grandmother tried to get each of her grandchildren, from the time we were young, to do past life regressions so we could remember who we were. I have always loved the jazz era of the 1950s, and when I regressed, that's where I popped up. I don't know exactly who I was, but I could see my body and sense where I was. I have two tattoos of that singers and scenes from that jazz era. I love tattoos as

a form of expression and have many thoughts about some
I'd love to have, but those are the only two I have chosen
to endure the for. They are tributes to Billie Holiday and
Nina Simone. I recently saw that the New Orleans,
Louisiana, airport is the Louis Armstrong Airport. I get
choked up, for no reason I know of, every time I hear the
name of that airport. That is likely a past life connection,
too.

*My Nina Simone tattoo. Art and tattoo by David Dettloff.
(http://inklab.com/david-dettloff/)*

We choose our lives. Yes, lives. Most of us are older souls
than we even realize. And if you're reading this book, you
are probably one of them. We also have souls that we

know. Dr. Michael Newton talks about how there are different levels of soul groups in his book *Journey of Souls*.

The people we love the most are probably our primary soul group, so to speak. The other people we know well are still people we have known in past lives, even the ones we hate. They are all here to help us along our path, and sometimes the people that hurt us the most are the ones that help adjust our course in the right directions.

Let me give you a couple examples. I recently was laid off from my corporate job of 15 years. A year and a half ago, I took a job in a different department because I liked the hiring leader. We had seen each other and knew of each other, and I just thought he was the nicest guy. The day he offered me the job, I clearly intended to go in and decline. Then I went in, however, and he said all the right things and I accepted it anyway, despite my first inclination not to accept.

There are no wrong choices, but you'll experience different things depending upon the direction you go. Suffice to say, the last 18 months I spent with the guy that I thought was so nice ended up being the wrong connection with a boss. We went together about as well as oil and water. Though I grew up at the company and loved all the other people I worked with, for whatever reason, he and I did not work together well. This ended up leading to my eventually leaving the company, not by my own choice. My position was eliminated.

At the same time, I had been putting off doing work as a psychic medium and author full-time for a while for fear of not having health insurance and a steady paycheck. I knew I was going to get there, I was just hesitant about pulling the trigger. So, instead of my listening to my own intuition, a choice was made for me beyond my control. Even though the time I spent in that role reporting to someone that made me uncomfortable most of the time was not a pleasant experience, it corrected my path to send me off in the direction I was supposed to go.

I also was born into a family that I loved very much but often wondered why I was with them. There was so much tribulation and misery, and I could not wait to escape them once I was of age. I was one of those kids that used to look up at the sky waiting for some unknown power to pick me up and take me away. I later came to realize that we chose each other for reasons that my human side may not understand but that my soul knows. I know that part of that reason was definitely to learn from each other.

Someone I know that had an abusive father who caused her a great deal of pain in this life. She then had a reading where he came through. In it, he talked about soul groups and the fact that before we live our life, we choose our different roles, kind of like people in a play. When there is the role of a villain, it is sometimes one of the most loving souls in the group that picks that role.

Since I wrote my first book *Gifted – A Guide for Mediums, Psychics & Intuitives*, my paternal grandmother read it cover to cover. She's one of the people I grew up in the same home with, and she and I have butted heads most of our lives. After she read the book, it opened her up to a few things. She even called the nuns on me to make sure what I was doing wasn't evil. (They assured her it wasn't and said they'd pray for me.) She's now in her nineties, and the closer it seems she gets to the end of her life, the more she reveals some very interesting insights.

As I left her house one night, she hugged me and told me how she loved me and that I was doing God's work as a medium. She then cried and said, "You're going to a different level of Heaven than me." At the moment, it surprised me, but later I realized it possibly aligns with the fact that we have different soul groups.

Purpose

One of the most frequent things I address during my psychic readings is the question: "What is my purpose?"

I think that we, as psychic mediums, all volunteered to be here on Earth just to help people because that's who we are. In doing so, we had to plan a life with our global purpose of helping others, sometimes just within our being. Then we had to plan a life for our personal reasons, the growth for our soul. Sometimes that growth is beautiful, and sometimes it's painful.

So many people I read for now are opening up to the fact that they are intuitive. Because I am a psychic medium, many of them realize they are mediums. A lot of them ask why they are just now opening up to this, especially when they are older. I assure them that was part of the plan they made for their lives: to live a life, to gain experience, and then to work at remembering what their soul knows.

Our purpose is love. All the rest is just being here to help others with our being. That may even be as simple as being kind to others. It may not be us being able to help everyone but being able to help one person at a time. If you are reading this book, you are a psychic medium and have the purpose of helping others with that gift. That does not mean it's your only purpose, although it is a lifetime of service.

Sometimes life doesn't turn out the way we planned. I always wanted to have a family— marriage and kids. Neither of those two things have turned out for me. Perhaps, that has all led me to this moment. Even though I don't understand it now, it's all part of my path which leads me to my purpose.

We may have forks in the road where we either get to decide which way to go or are sometimes forced in the direction we go. We may have experiences when we nearly lose our lives or have other life events that scare us and make us realize that we need to make a change. When I lost my day job, I realized there were certain priorities I had to get in order. I had to see the people I loved more, which included a trip to Boston to see one of my best friends. I had to take charge of my health, including getting my ankle healed because I had a problem with torn tendons.

Sometimes hard times are the things in life that push us towards our purpose. Regardless of what our purpose is, it will always find us. In fact, most of our purpose has already been accomplished by us just being born.

CHAPTER 10: DEPRESSION, ANXIETY, AND LONELINESS

Depression and Anxiety

Many of us suffer from depression, anxiety, or both. I have suffered from them both on and off. When I was about 18 years old, I had anxiety attacks. That was also the same age when the ability to sense Spirit I had suppressed came back. That return was not the reason I was diagnosed with anxiety, but I'm sure that somewhere in my soul I knew something needed to be done, and I was anxious over the fact that I had not gotten there yet.

I started seeing a therapist before I got divorced, and I have been seeing her on and off for about 15 years. I had a bad bout with depression in 2014. I have always had a knowing that it was not my purpose to die by my own hand, but when I started having suicidal thoughts, they escalated. They went from "I don't want to be here anymore" to "I want to kill myself" to starting to plan it. I had felt so blue for so long, and when my suicidal thoughts became that specific, I knew that I needed additional help. I knew it wasn't me talking; it was the depression.

I went in thinking I'd be diagnosed with mild depression. When my therapist told me all the symptoms, I had nearly all of them. At that time, I was diagnosed with moderate depression. I fought it without medication for a while, but when the depression wasn't getting better, it evolved into anxiety, which didn't feel that much better to me. Then I had a trigger in my life that made me finally consent to medication. I had really not wanted to, but I thought my life was too important not to. I was tired of being miserable.

I'm getting better now, but it's a daily choice to do so. Let's be honest, it's hard to live on Earth and feel all the intensity of being here. There are injustices, murder, war, and more.

Going through what I did made me thankful that it wasn't worse. I sometimes forget I'm human and try to do too much and rush life. One thing I do too much of is move my home. I think I'm never quite comfortable and keep looking for the next comfortable place to live because the home I'm looking for doesn't have the comfort of the one my soul remembers in Heaven. The question is: How do I live with myself?

As I mentioned earlier, I recently lost my job, and I started to have anxiety attacks again. I hadn't had anxiety attacks since I was diagnosed with PTSD at the age of 19 (from being the victim of violent crimes). I thought I was over that sort of thing, and I found myself just brushing off the symptoms, such as heart palpitations and shortness of breath. I'd recently had an EKG (heart test) and knew my heart was fine, so I finally realized that this had to be anxiety and went on medication for that as well.

During a reading with one of my regular clients, she kept trying to direct the reading in a specific direction, and I suddenly started having the anxiety attack feelings in my body. I asked if she had this problem. She verified it. I said that I felt she had medication for it as well, which she also verified. I asked her why she wasn't taking her medication for it, and she said she did, but only to sleep. I then explained to her that her guides were saying that the medication was for whenever she felt anxiety attacks and not just for sleeping.

Does this type of depression or anxiety sound familiar? Have you had worse? Do you have a condition that needs constant support and medication? I believe that we've been shamed into not talking about this, but so many psychic mediums have battled this at one time or the other because we know there are so many people that need help and we can't help them fast enough.

We were also born sensitive souls. It's hard for us to feel the problems that happen on Earth and not be able to control them or help everyone. We live on a very violent planet.

Know that you are not alone. If you have been trying everything natural to help the depression or anxiety and it's not working like it should be, it may be time to talk to a health professional and consider medication. It has helped me, and it helps others, too. It will not make you less of a person or less of a psychic medium. In fact, once you feel less of the depression or anxiety, you may be in a better place to help others and more compassionate because you have been through the same thing as many of your clients.

Loneliness

Ever since the day I was born, I have felt lonely. I had a loving family and all of the human love I could want, but there were some days that I felt like I didn't belong here. I wanted to be normal. It took me so long to realize that the last thing I am is normal, and that's not what I—or we— are supposed to be.

So much of the struggle with psychic mediums is just in accepting the gift, let alone developing it and helping others with it. We may get satisfaction out of the service that we provide to others. Then we go back to our life outside of helping people, and sometimes the loneliness sets in.

I believe that loneliness is the separation of our soul from Heaven. I think so many of us volunteered to come to this planet, but perhaps we hadn't been on the Earth or lived a life for a while. It was our wise soul, however, that was required in helping others on this Earth, either by giving them a reading or by helping them in some other way.

I have loved, I have lost, and I have chosen to live alone at this point in my life. It is just me and my pets; I like it that way. I have learned the very human lesson of knowing that it's better to be alone than to wish you were alone. That said, the loneliness that I think we all feel is the one in our very core which we can't explain, but it is just there like an ache and we don't know what to do with it.

As a result of this loneliness, sometimes we imbibe or do something that makes us forget. That masks the pain of being lonely. We go through depression or anxiety, we gain weight we didn't want, and worst of all, we have to deal with our human ailments. We don't understand why we must go through such loneliness because we know we are here to do good: we have chosen to come to Earth to help others. The way we help the most is by having a body. That is our blessed vessel to do this work. It's hard for us to stop and listen to our bodies, but when we don't, that is when we break down. I know you understand.

I sit here writing this with a boot on my right leg. I had surgery this week for a torn tendon in my ankle. It took over a year and two doctors to figure out what was wrong, and then I thought I was finally going to have surgery to fix it. I knew the doctor would find something worse than what he originally thought, but the one thing that never occurred to me is was that it would be so bad that the doctor would close me up without doing anything to help me because he couldn't do anything in that first surgery. He'd never seen that kind of tear before, so I now have to heal from this failed attempt and then go back for another surgery. I am grateful because it could be so much worse, but it's still a total disappointment and an immense amount of pain to cope with.

I think it's hard for us to accept our humanity, and that leads to the loneliness. No one can tell you what you to do with your struggle to be human or the loneliness it can bring, but I need you to know that you are not alone. The key is to figure out how to remedy it. Is it learning to do readings? Is it acting on the thought you have had about making a change to your relationship? Is it getting a divorce? Is it going out to have fun for a night?

I used to worry about so many things that could harm me, such as food, smoking, and the like. Now I realize that I have to do what I enjoy because something is bound to kill me. We are all going home at some point, but none of us know when or how that might be. So, we have to learn to let go, live our lives, and try not to completely succumb to the loneliness.

CHAPTER 11: THE CHANNELED MESSAGES

The following are messages I was guided to channel for this book. When I first felt guided to do this, I was specifically told there would be three messages, and those are the messages that follow. The messages are channeled primarily from my own spiritual team—my spirit guides, angels, and so on. There is one specific message where it is "signed," so to speak, that says who channeled the message through me.

Channeled Message One

Dear Ones,

We plead with you right now not to abandon your purpose. Many of you are wondering why you are here. We beg you to please have faith and remember the reason why you volunteered to be here right now. You are old, wise souls who have seen the harm to the Earth and its inhabitants over time. You have been many things in other lifetimes, as well as when you were "home," which many of you call Heaven.

You answered a call that the universe, God, or whatever your higher power was asked you to consider, to help the people on Earth. You have seen so many things that you have felt helpless about. You thought you were done, and as such, you also think you may graduate after this life. You always have free will, but, in fact, you are such loving souls that you have chosen to be in a body time after time to help others.

Many of you have been behind the scenes trying to guide other people as a spirit guide or something of the like in other roles or lifetimes. You knew that you were not always heard because the human you were guiding could not or chose not to listen. Thus, the biggest difference you could create was being on Earth right now.

There are so many things that we could say to you in human terms, but we don't want to isolate you more. "Wake up" is the least of what we have to say. Please stop doubting that you are special, that you have gifts which you don't pay heed to or don't want to be exposed.

You are here to help one another. Please have faith that while it's not the only reason you are here, it's one of your many purposes in this life to help others.

That means the time is now. It's time to wake up and stop doubting what the Creator has called you to do. You are abundant, and you have all the gifts you have had with you over many lifetimes. You can choose to isolate yourself or hide behind other things, as you ultimately do have free will. When you do this, however, you may not be able to fully realize your life's purpose. That makes you feel empty.

The trick, as you say on Earth, is to try to have fun, relax, and enjoy life when you are not helping others. As a giving soul, that is hard for you. We understand. But life is short; it's not just a saying. When you inhabit a body, you feel as if it's forever when, in fact, it's only a blip in the time you are here.

You ask about soul groups or wonder why you are with the family that you are with, why you have incarnated here with these people at this special time. Many of you have chosen to help the people you have incarnated with and, in doing so, have chosen to be the helper which means sometimes being the victim or the abused. You are no longer the victim, but we have heard your questions and have wanted to answer them. Everything you have gone through has led to this moment right now.

We need for you to wake up and realize that you are special. You are beloved, and you are a gem in the eyes of the Creator. You are no mistake. The only mistake is in turning the other cheek and ignoring how special you are. You were created in His image: never doubt that.

You have done no wrong. Please stop being so hard on yourselves. You are authentic in your life, your experiences, and your gifts. Please have confidence to learn more, help others, and share what you know in the matters of Spirit.

You have this gift because you can. You can connect to Heaven in a way that not many can. So please trust that we would not ask unless you could deliver the answer that others need to hear. You are sought for your gifts. Please believe that you are the answer that so many others seek.

Channeled Message Two

SUICIDE

This is something that rests so heavy on your mind, dear one. You have seen people you love, or that have touched you in some way, leave this Earth by their own hand. You may have had someone you love dearly that left the Earth by their own hand. You may even be thinking about why you want to leave this Earth yourself.

First, we want to address those of you who are suicidal. We cannot overlook depression and want you to know that if you feel suicidal, please address this with those that love you or a health professional. If you are already in the planning stage and reading this right now, this is your sign that we beg you to please reconsider. You are very needed on this Earth right now, and you are loved more than you could possibly imagine. We promise that not all moments are going to feel worth it, but your presence on this planet is very worthwhile, or the Creator would not have made you in His divine image.

You may feel very alone or feel that you have betrayed yourself or others in some way, but these things shall pass. Please hold your head high and know that you are loved. You feel this way, in part, because you sense that your true home may not feel like it's here on Earth. We cannot tell you all that exists back home in Heaven, or you would never stay to do the mission that you signed up to do.

We cannot give you all the answers, but please know that we know and feel your every move, trouble, sadness, and all the things you think you have done wrong. You have done nothing wrong in the eyes of the Creator. Please know that we mean you—the very person reading this right now. We love you and cheer you on to the mission you have before you, no matter what you choose. There is no wrong answer, just an answer that will alter things one way or the other.

Those who have taken their own lives are not stuck in limbo. They do not go to Hell. They just had an exit point in their life—that was pre-chosen before they lived—in which they could leave Earth if they wanted to. Those that leave on their own decision have done nothing wrong in the eyes of God, so please don't worry about their souls.

They are safe with their Creator and still choose their path and what happens next. They have ascended home to Heaven.

Channeled Message Three

The time has come for you to awaken to open your arms to the gifts you have and allow yourselves to receive. We have loved you and watched you for a very long time, longer perhaps than you know in this life.

There are some of you that had very difficult paths in this life, and we have been here to support you every step of the way, even though you did not realize it. There are so many things you do not know and want answers to, and we will try to explain that in the best way we can.

Ask for our help. We may not give you the exact answer you seek, but sometimes when you seek help, you don't always get the answer you want but what you need. So many of you reading this already ask for our help, and sometimes do not see the sign, feel it, or get the message in the way you expect. If you are having a hard time doing so, please ask us for a sign that you can understand and then believe the things that happen that you tend to brush off as phenomena.

Some of you cry to us that life is hard, and you want to come home. We know, and we cry with you when that happens. We so want to comfort you and tell you that it is going to be okay. You make no mistakes, our loved ones, so please forgive yourself now. You have old souls, and as a result, you are sometimes perfectionists, impatient, or many other human things. You know that you know things, and you are striving to remember all that your soul knows.

When you came to this life, you planned it. We know you may not think that, and we are sorry if we upset you and it hurts you to think about that. Think of it, perhaps, in another way: you asked God for an assignment. With all the love you have in your soul, many of you volunteered to do that very thing to help this Earth out now. Please realize that some of you have accomplished that just in being born and living life to this point. We don't mean to be trite, but sometimes the answer is not what you expect, you see?

Please understand that you needed this body to be who you are. It is your vessel. It is sometimes heavy and hurts you with its ailments, including the addiction, anxiety, and depression you worry about and that make you wonder what is wrong with you. Nothing is wrong with you in God's eyes, for He is the true Creator of all, and that includes you.

You inherently know that you came to Earth to do something, and some of you now feel empty because you still haven't figured it out. Remember that, perhaps, helping others is in doing so one person at a time. If you do not know what step is next, do not worry: you will feel it. In many cases, the things that you desire fall into your lap when you accept or decide upon them.

We know you grow tired now. You sometimes feel as if you are going around and around in circles on a ride that you want to get off. You wanted a family and didn't have one. You had other plans for your life, and they somehow didn't materialize. Thank you for having faith despite your hurt and knowing that there was a plan, even if you do not yet know what it is.

Slow down. All the things you wish do not come over night. Ask us for assistance. We are here with you always.

The Archangels Michael, Nathaniel, Uriel, Gabriel, and Metatron

CHAPTER 12: A MESSAGE FOR INTUITIVE CHILDREN

I know that you may feel very sensitive. You may be able to sense the presence of Spirit all around you. It's intense for you to go school, shopping malls, or other crowded places. You see or feel Spirit all the time. Sometimes the ghosts might try to talk to you. This happened to me and to many others like us when we were young.

You may feel that the sense of Spirit is most intense at night. You feel them more strongly right as you are about to go to bed, or you may even feel like you can't sleep because you don't know how to make them go away. There are many reasons for this. You are more open as a child, and while that may never go away, it's most frightening or overwhelming at that time because you don't know how to stop it or know what to do. You may not know how to deliver the messages that you feel like they have for you because you really can't hear them, or you may not know who to deliver the message to.

If this sounds like you, you are not alone. There are many things you can do to protect or shield yourself from this.

Ask Your Angels for Help

You always have angels around you—good angels. You may have heard of the term "guardian angel," and it's true that you have one. They may protect you from accidents or something that might hurt you.

The rest of the angels are also around you. They see your hurt, sense your fear, and comfort you when you cry. If you are afraid of the spirits or paranormal activity that you sense/feel/hear around you, please ask the angels for help.

If you are at home, ask Archangel Michael (St. Michael) to come in and clear out all the spirits from you that aren't for your greatest and highest good. Ask him to place windows for them to leave through at all the doors and windows in your home. He will lovingly do that. If you ask, don't worry that you might be taking him away from someone else, for he is omnipresent, meaning he can be many places at once. He would love you to ask him for help.

The angels around you can only help if you ask, and they would love it if you do so more often. You don't have to say it aloud: say it in your head, and they will answer. If you need more concrete proof that they are there, either ask them for a sign of their presence or assistance that you will easily understand, or even ask them to come closer to you so you can feel their presence. You will be amazed at all the unconditional love you feel when that happens.

Night Time Protection

One thing that I do myself and recommend to others is to imagine the following. I see my bed in my mind and imagine it with mirrors all around and above it that face outwards. Mirrors facing outward deflect negative energy.

I did this once in a home where I felt lots of Spirit activity. I woke up in the middle of the night and saw spirits that were bouncing off the space surrounding the bed as though they were not able to penetrate the shield of mirrors.

Spirits know you can sense, or even see, them. They are not typically here to do anything bad, so don't worry. Tell God that you only want what is for your greatest good in that regard.

As psychic mediums, we always sense Spirit and always have spirits around us, so please try not to get frustrated. There are just some people who have passed who want to communicate with the living, and they sense you can do that, even if you do not know you can yet.

Energy

As a highly intuitive individual, you are inclined to pick up the energy of those around you. You may sometimes even pick it up from shows you see, music you hear, or the video games you play. That doesn't mean you should not do what you enjoy, only that you should be aware that when you feel heavy energetically (having a bad day and don't know why, don't know why you're feeling groggy), it's time to ask your angels to help you. Ask your angels, especially Archangel Michael, to cut your energetic cords and clear away any energy that is not for your greatest and highest good from head to toe. Energetic cords are something you might pick up when you are out. Others may sense your healing energy and unknowingly attach a cord to you because they like your energy. It's not bad: it's just that it might weight you down emotionally. It's easy to just ask your angels for help in clearing you and cutting those cords.

Old Soul

You may have been told you were an old soul, or you may

feel like one. You are. You came to Earth to help others because the Earth needed help. You may get angry sometimes or feel like you know more than others. You have to do your best to play your earthly role in the kindest way you can so that you can help people.

For most of you, it's just your job to grow up and to use some of these tools to assist you when you feel frustrated or afraid because of all that you sense and feel. It doesn't mean you can't learn about some of these things. The more you learn, the more you will be able to tune out or even control some of the things that overwhelm you.

Remember you are here with great purpose. You are loved from Heaven above just for being here. Have faith that your purpose will reveal itself as time goes on.

CHAPTER 13: THE BUSINESS SECTION

The reasons that are driving me to write this business section is that I have so many peers and so many clients that want to start their own business to do something they love. That means, perhaps, a metaphysical bookstore, a healing center, or another school or center to do readings, classes, or the like.

The issue is that we sometimes think that God is going to do the work for us once we start or that we can "put it out to the universe" and the details will follow. I had a reading with a woman recently who said she wanted to open a healing center. I asked her if she had done any healing work, and she said she had not. I then asked her if she had a business plan, and she didn't. While she might have good intentions, she was not taking steps to make her dream happen.

I've also read other books that skip this type of information or don't address it thoroughly. I'm not sure if I can cover everything that could be covered, but I worked in the realm of finance for nearly 20 years. I've been grateful for that when I have thought about starting my own spiritual practice, and I want to share what I know with you and at least give you some action steps that will help you along the way.

I want to make it clear before I begin that I am not an attorney or tax advisor and that all of what I am telling you is from the point of view of starting a business in the country I live in, the United States. I think that many of the things I say will be applicable and translatable, but you should always consider consulting a professional tax advisor, attorney, or other applicable professional when making business decisions.

We may want to do spiritual work and help others, but, as with anything, this is also a business. When I started out in this field, I was not sure I'd make any money, but things have changed. My work is evolving into a full-time business for me, so now I work with a tax advisor to help me sort through and file my taxes every year. This may be something you will want to consider as you move forward, as well.

Building Your Brand

You may have had a job before, but you never have had the career of your dreams. Well, you CAN have the career of your dreams: you just must make sure you put in the work to get there before you start working. You cannot jump right in and expect it to fly off the ground and cover all the bills. It will get there eventually, if all goes well, but you must co-create your business with Spirit, and part of that creation is your brand.

To build a name for yourself is the epitome of building your brand. Everything you do is your brand. If you are someone that is always late, that becomes part of your brand because everyone then knows you as the person who's always running late. If you tend to be the life of the party, that also is a part of your brand because that's what people associate with your name when they hear it.

When I first began giving readings, no one knew who I was. I was lucky enough to have someone to give me a platform by letting me do free readings and advertising those free readings to her clientele. It ultimately confirmed to me that I could actually do this work.

After those first free readings, I started doing events as I could, and that evolved into private readings and so forth. I started doing psychic fairs and psychic expos. One of the first times I did a psychic expo, however, I made a bit of a mistake. I bought a booth from someone that could no longer do the event. She was one of my peers in the psychic world, but she'd been doing this work much longer than I had and, thus, had her own brand. The event was not the normal sort of psychic expo I now do; it was geared more toward paranormal investigators. I also did not realize that there were several VIP mediums giving readings at the event. I met some great people there, but I didn't do too many readings. Suffice to say, I did not make my money back for that event.

Now that I have been doing this work for a while and have written a book or two, I have established my own brand. I believe the important parts of my brand will remain constant, but the brand itself will continue to evolve as my journey moves forward and I grow and change.

If you want to start your own spiritual business, the first thing you want to think about is brand building. First of all, you need to consider what you want your professional brand to be. To do this, you need to figure out what your personal brand is.

When I think about my personal (just Lisa) brand, it probably contains the following:

- Loud
- Intense
- Talkative

- Authentic
- Independent
- Self-sufficient

What words would you used to describe yourself? What words do you think others might use to describe you? Make a list of those words. That's your personal brand.

Now that you see what makes up your personal brand, it's time to think about what you'd like to mold into your professional brand. Do you want to be the nice medium, the truthful medium, the psychic from your area or city, or so forth? Your brand is also about what kind of work you want to do. Do you want to do private sittings? Will your business start online? Even if you aren't sure where to start, or aren't even out there doing readings right now, it's still never too early to start thinking about your brand.

Marketing

When I went to release my first book, *Gifted – A Guide for Mediums, Psychics & Intuitives*, I wanted to somehow create a buzz for this book in advance of the book. I started to talk about it online, and I also started a YouTube channel where I did some free oracle card readings. With each new book, I added more ways to get the word out. I also now pre-release the cover of each new book on social media. I then follow that up with teaser passages from the book.

If you are not writing a book, then do things like a daily message or reading. Social media is key because, like it or not, that's where people spend a lot of their time. Think of how many positive messages that you've seen on social media that have meant something to you. Also, think about all the social media sites out there, not just the ones you like. Everyone is different, and you want to make sure you get your message out to as many people as possible.

You can have a logo made to go with your brand. I had one made by Regina Wamba at Mae I Design (http://www.maeidesign.com). She does most of my book covers and also designs logos. We worked together to come up with an idea, and the image below is how it turned out. I had the "II" placed in the middle of the wings for Gemini, my sun sign.

LISA ANDRES

AUTHOR AND PSYCHIC MEDIUM

If you are just starting out and on a budget and do not know how to do this sort of thing yourself, you can have a logo made on the freelancer website called Fiverr (https://www.fiverr.com/). This site offers cost-effective branding, logo, and graphic design options. I have had a few little things done there, but I make sure I look at the ratings of the person and ask questions before I book the job. Overall, I have had good experiences with the freelancers on that site.

I have an ongoing Facebook marketing campaign called Brand Building that I pay for. There are lots of options for marketing, and you don't have to pay for them all. Your job is just to start getting the word out there about you.

If marketing is not your thing, you're either going to have to fake it until you make it or think about asking someone that's good at it for help. One good book I read on this subject was *Platform: Getting Noticed in a Noisy World* by Michael Hyatt. It may be of help to you.

Advertising

Over the years I have tried many different advertising tactics. In my area, we have a local printed and digital version of a metaphysical newspaper/magazine. At first, I ran a monthly ad in their section of listed businesses in the area. Then I paid for an ad run on a "Best Psychics" type of website. I stopped doing all of that for a while when I was part-time because a lot of my business seems to come from client referrals, or word of mouth. I ask clients where they found me. At this point, most say they heard about me from someone or read my book. Now that I am going to be full-time, I'm going to again have a monthly ad in my local metaphysical paper to help gain more exposure.

You can also do a lot of advertising on social media for free. Make sure that this is something you don't overlook. The best thing that you can do is to try things out to see what works best for you, but I would say the best way to advertise is really just to get out there and start working to build your brand.

Website

I also had a website designed and created. There are lots of free websites available or ways to create your own website at a low cost. I decided that, for me, when my book came out, I wanted a professional online presence. I checked out several peers' websites for ideas. I eventually found the perfect web designers that worked with me to create what I wanted, and I felt that they gave a fair price. They also worked with me on a payment plan, which really helped.

I have seen some of my peers that use free website platforms that have fantastic websites, so there's no limit to what you can do. The big thing is that you MUST have a website—no exceptions. Even if that is not your thing, we live in a world where the fastest way that people can find something out is to do an Internet search for it. A website is almost essential for people to find you through that method.

Business Cards

You must have business cards, and they are pretty easy to get. I had my web designers design the card template to be consistent with the design of my website. One thing I like is for mine is to have my picture on the cards. The reason I have my picture on my card is because I thought of all the business cards that people pick up at events. I feel that it would be easier for prospective clients to remember me if they have a picture.

I have trade show signs for when I do public events, such as psychic expos. I have a big one for bigger shows and a smaller one that sits on my table when I'm at a smaller event. When I'm at a bigger event, I bring a sign that gives a little biographical information about me because a lot of people might ask what I do or what a psychic medium is.

For my table at the events where I do several readings in a day, I have branded (Lisa Andres) marketing material. I have pens out with my name, logo, and website on them for people to sign in, as well as extras so they can take one with them. That's good advertising. I also have small pads of paper with my picture, my name, my title, and my website on them. I give them to clients at public events to use during readings. That way they can take notes during their reading, or I can write down notes for them about something that came up during the reading, such as suggested books. This, too, allows them to leave with something that has my name and information on it.

Getting Out There: Events and Readings

If you are someone that is very afraid to come out of the psychic closet, so to speak, you're not alone. Start slow.

You can always do this work under another name and/or do it solely via the Web. I met one woman who told me she was a pet communicator, and she thought that no one in her small town would buy into that. She got a website and now has clients all over the country. Her neighbors are none the wiser. I also have a few clients who have practiced under pen names, so to speak, and I would suggest that option to anyone who is struggling with the decision to go public.

If you do use a different name, check to see what the policy on working under a different name is where you live. For instance, in the state I live in, you have to register the alternate name with the state. That is something to think about, especially if you get to the point where you are doing this on a more full-time basis and earning money from it.

I touched on this earlier, but when I started, I didn't know what to do. I learned how to lose money quickly by paying for a show or two where the real attraction wasn't the psychics, readers, or healers. I recommend you make sure that you avoid doing something like that. If you are a woman, then a woman's expo may work, but I'd still say to err on the side of caution and stick to the fairs that are commonly for psychic mediums and have the energy you want. If you buy a booth at a home and garden show, however, you may not be very busy because that's not what the people walking through the door are typically there for.

In my early days of brand building, if I wasn't busy, I would run a special where I would lower my price for a reading. In that way, I had people I was helping even in slow times, and they also helped pay expenses. It may be tempting to do free readings to get more people in your booth, but remember that you are worthy of being paid for your time. Not everyone is able to do what we do. While it's nice to think about giving your services away, you should try to charge for readings, especially if you're trying to build a business. If you really want to give away a reading, you could do a giveaway where you have a signup sheet for a chance to win a free reading if the person signs up for your email list.

There's one great website that I go to that has lots of psychic festivals and things around the world in this field. It is called Mind, Body, Spirit Events (http://www.bodymindspiritdirectory.org/FindExpos.htm l). Not everyone is on it because vendors have to pay to be on there, but it's still a really good resource.

When you are just starting out, keep it local. The most powerful thing you can do is build a brand and gather your following locally. I didn't know that's what I was doing the first few years I did this type of work, but staying in the market I live in, which luckily has a lot of events, really helped me to build a following.

As I evolved into teaching, I started asking friends who had their own metaphysical centers for opportunities. It was nice but also competitive to get a spot, especially if the price was reasonable, since the calendar was typically full. Now I've started to use a nearby hotel meeting room for classes. I called around and negotiated until I got the price I wanted. For example, I started out saying I'd have about 25 people. They quoted me about twice what I wanted to pay, so I lowered it to 10 to 12 people, and that got the price I wanted at a place that was near to me but still central to most people in the area I live in. Then I advertised that event as "class space limited" and had a full classroom of students. I could give more one-on-one attention, too, because it was smaller.

When you do plan an event, advertise it. That's typically been the only time I pay for an ad in a local metaphysical magazine while working part-time. You will also want to make flyers to hand out at events if you do something like psychic fairs. If you know someone that has a metaphysical fair or shop, ask if you can leave flyers or advertise there, as well.

After a few years, having established myself in my local market, I then experimented with traveling outside my local area. I started small by traveling to other areas in my state that had a decent metropolitan size. The events I did were hit-or-miss, and I had to take stock of what these travels were really meant to do. I realized that the less successful events were not well-advertised, so I now check to be sure that the events are well-advertised by the event's chairperson before I make plans to go.

I also go with my intuition. I kept getting the feeling I needed to go to Omaha, Nebraska, which is about 500 miles away from me. I had no idea what event to do there, and I just gave it up to the universe that if I was supposed to go, I'd go. It took over a year, but I finally found what felt right and took a chance in going there to try to further my reach. I met some of the best people there, both peers and people that I have helped. I'm now building a brand there, and I will go back to that event for the third time next year.

One year, I decided that one of my local events I had been doing for years was getting too expensive because of the metropolitan area I live in. I saw an ad for a psychic expo in Iowa City, Iowa, which is about a five-hour drive for me. The price tag was just right, and I took the leap of faith and made the reservation. It was entirely different, both in the clients I had and the building we were in, but I loved it there. I loved the people, and now I know there is a reason I felt like going there. I will keep doing that event going forward, as long as I feel guided to.

If you are thinking about traveling for an event, ask your peers. Some of them might have already tried some of the events you are thinking about and might have some insight. I have definitely decided not to go to certain events or areas based on what I've heard from my peers.

It's sometimes difficult to take a leap of faith, whether it's doing an event where you aren't sure there will be many people, holding a class for the first time, or traveling on a larger geographic scale. Remember: you don't have to do this all at once. Start small. Find your comfort level. You may eventually push beyond your comfort zone a bit, but this business is so much in the gray area, as opposed to the black and white, that it is best to just go where you feel guided. Start local and stay there for a while. Then see how it goes from there.

Parties

I was first asked to do readings at a party by a person that started as a private client for me, which meant that she wanted to have several friends over to her house to each receive a private reading from me. She now has hosted several such parties, and I have enjoyed that work and met some wonderful people along the way.

Parties can be a good way to expand your reach and build your name. It can also teach you that you have to have boundaries with the guests and the host or hostess. Make sure you say what you need. Is it a certain amount of money? A deposit in advance? An upcharge if the travel is more than a certain number of miles? I limit my travel for parties to my local metropolitan area, but I will consider an upcharge if it's further than that.

In doing parties, I have also learned that you need a minimum amount of people there so that you get the money you need for the event. Yes, it's not all about the money, but it's still a business. I typically say there must be eight to twelve people there. That will keep me working for about four hours. It's also highly unlikely twelve people will show up since there are usually some cancellations at the last minute, just like with any party.

Group Readings

To me, a group reading means an event where I read live for a group. There can be 25 or more people there, and not everyone is guaranteed a reading. I still charge everyone and disclose that a reading is not guaranteed in the event. You can also charge a minimum fee for appearances like this.

Advertise on your website that you are available for live audience readings. You can organize these events just like you'd organize a class or any other event you have. You can choose the venue if you organize the event yourself, or you can ask your potential client to do that if you are approached about doing a group reading.

Speaking at Events

A lot of the events I do have mini-classes during the day. If you are paying to be there, you can offer to do a class at no extra charge. That can be a good way to build a following and fill in extra time that you might have at slower events. If it's an event, however, where you are there to make enough money to pay for your costs and need to do as many readings as possible to do so, you may not want to teach a class because it will take you away from the readings you make money doing.

The more I do this work, the more I am asked to do events. I have been asked to be a vendor who purchases a table or booth, and I have even been asked to be a keynote speaker a time or two. I have turned down many of these opportunities because I either didn't want to travel to where the event was or didn't hear good things about the event. The best thing you can do is ask your peers what their experiences have been with a certain show. What they say will help you decide.

Keynote speakers typically get paid, whether it is with a free booth at an event, a room, or something else. If you are a bit more well-known, you could also be paid a monetary sum. I did a keynote event where I allowed them to refund the cost I had paid for my booth in exchange for a keynote spot. I chose to do that because I liked that event and did not mind being associated with being the keynote speaker. Again, this goes back to being choosy about the events you choose to do in the first place

You might read this and think you'll never get to the point where you will be a speaker at an event, but I was once just like you. I have grown and learned so much, and you will, too. I have successful peers that have been doing this longer than me that now travel the world speaking at and doing these events, and they typically are paid for it and have paid travel arrangements. While this has not happened for me yet, I know that it will if it is meant to be.

It may take you a while to get up the courage to speak at an event. Public speaking is a fear for many people. Just remember that if you have the opportunity to do this or are asked, then there are probably people that would benefit from what you have to say.

Email

One thing that is important to do is to create an email for your business and then find a service such as Mailchimp or Constant Contact that you allow you to do mass emails, both routinely and to "blast out" to your clients when you have an event. These services typically can give you insight into how your emails are doing as well, such as who's clicking your links, which links are being clicked, and who is subscribing or unsubscribing to your mailing list.

I have a signup link on my website for my email list, and I also take a signup sheet to my events for people that want my emails. One thing about email lists in the United States is that you must put an address on the email footer. I don't want my own address on my emails, so I rent a post office box. That way I can not only use the PO address for that, but I can also dedicate it to mail for my business.

Try to send out at least a monthly email. You can develop a strategy of what you want to say or what you want to advertise in it. You might be able to attach a video of you talking, add intuitive messages, or something like that. That will also help build your brand and potentially your following.

Tax Person or Accountant

Self-employment taxes can be a challenge. You may get paid cash or through something that takes credit cards like Square or PayPal. I decided to have a paid person help me make sure I'm filing correctly, and I keep an Excel spreadsheet all year of my expenses and earnings, as well as mileage for my car. I was referred to the person I work with by a friend who was self-employed, so do your research into who you hire. I absolutely would not do it any other way. Since I worked in finance for many years, I was really good at doing my own taxes, even if they were somewhat complex. I stopped when I began to have self-employment income and royalties for books. There were all sorts of tax schedules and things I didn't understand, so I wanted to make sure I was doing my taxes correctly.

Leasing a Space or Office

It's up to you to decide if you want to have a home-based business, which is what I do at this time. Most of my private readings are done over the phone. At this point, in my own business, I don't want the cost of rent and utilities associated with having an outside office. If someone wants to see you in person and you feel that holds more value, you can always do a reading in a coffee shop or public space like a park if needed. I have done that before. You could also rent a place for a short time if needed.

Perhaps, it's still your dream to open up your own store or metaphysical center. Just be sure to do your research before doing so. In the United States, corporate leases are typically lengthy. I have known people who leased space and were successful, but I have also known those who have not been successful with it and went broke over it and had to give up their dream and go back to a traditional job. It depends on what you want to do, having the right business partners to work with you, and what products you are going to have. For example, whether or not you are going to have a healer or tarot card reader work with you are things that might help or hinder your business's success based on what you were trying to achieve.

Just know that if you open a store, you may have to be somewhat married to it. Decide what you want and how many hours you want to be there before you make that sort of commitment. Also, work your way up to opening a store after you've built a brand and following so that it's not such a challenge getting business in the door.

Loss of Mentors

What do you do when one of your teachers leaves this business? Perhaps, it's a sign for you to start teaching. One of my first teachers recently became a born-again Christian. I can respect that, but it was hard for me and some of her other students because that meant that she no longer believed the things she used to write about or teach. I will always love this person, but I took the news hard. I loved listening to her and being led by her, but it was her time to stop or, perhaps, even retire from what she'd been doing for so long.

When things like that happen, it's time for other energy to step into that space. Maybe you can help do that by continuing, or starting, to do this work.

Some Final Thoughts on Getting Started in This Business

After losing my corporate job, I thought back to when I got my first hint that it was time to leave. I realized that so many of my peers had something similar happen to them before they started doing this work full-time. They either quit or lost their job and then decided to put more energy into being a psychic medium, and it gradually took off. I feel that, perhaps, we lost those jobs so we would not be spending our time in a toxic work environment anymore and are not being held down by that. I know that the universe is pointing me in the direction of my dreams and giving me the opportunity to slowly turn those dreams into a reality.

Now that I have the time, I will be putting more energy into a private practice. For me, that's mostly doing private readings via phone, and maybe, at some point, I will do them via Skype as well. I will continue to do events like psychic expos, but, as before, I will still be choosy about the ones I do. I have learned that from experience.

The one thing I feel like I have not put enough energy into is teaching others. I do some of that in the books I write, and when I was working full-time, I was teaching about twice a year. I know that there are people out there hungry to learn and that I can teach more. Primarily, I have only taught mediums. I usually advise new mediums to take psychic development classes so that they can learn how to use their psychic tools. I have always thought I should try to teach my own version of psychic development someday, and this seems to be my opportunity. At the time of writing this book, I feel like I should offer a couple of weekday classes. That's something that I am not sure about because so many potential students work during the day, but even I have to have faith and just go as I'm guided.

Know that if this happens to you as it has me, it's a nudge from the universe. Even if you decide to go to another job, you still have a chance. If you are in a position where you don't know how to leave your full-time job, put your desire out to the universe and stop trying to force it. When you force something, you tend to thwart progress.

I have had many people ask me in readings if they could do this business full-time and leave their jobs. I tend to ask them if they have done this type of work before, and they generally say they haven't. Then I ask if they have run a business before, and they also say they haven't. We then proceed to talk about the things in this chapter.

If you find yourself wanting to do this full-time but have not done this work or ran a business, start by doing this type of work. That's the most important thing. You do not have to be perfect to do this, either in your own life or when you do the readings. It's a job of service, and it's your job to go where you are led.

If you are still wondering how to get started, please just do it. The world needs you now, not when you are perfect or the master of your craft. That doesn't mean you shouldn't continue to study and learn more: it means that you won't get experience unless you try. You WILL get the word "no" when you ask a question sometimes; most of us do. Being a good psychic medium is delivering correct messages most of the time, not all of the time. If it is a "no," let it be a "no." Try to maybe rephrase what you heard, but if it's a "no" again, move on. The information will come back if it's supposed to.

When you start to do readings, you are starting to build your brand, which will ultimately be built with time. Take baby steps. Go as you are guided. No one is going to give you the answers about what to do; only you know that. There's no express path to building your own business. You must first start doing the work and then let the universe guide you through the next steps. As I've said before, don't force it. Be gentle with yourself, and if you are brand new to this, try to be patient.

If you are in the United Kingdom, you could start as a medium at a church service in a Spiritualist Church. When I attended Arthur Findlay College in the UK, I learned that many mediums there work in churches. That's not something we have as much of where I live, so we have to find opportunities or create them.

As I have said, I was once where you are. We're all at different levels in our development. I'm not perfect, and neither should you be. I have had some of my teachers say that they had to have a certain length waiting list of readings before they would quit their day jobs. Others have asked Spirit and been told they didn't have to quit work but would have plenty of clients if they did. You have to make the decision on when the time is right for you. Most importantly, don't just quit your primary source of income without a plan. Start with baby steps and put more energy into it as you go along. It may take off more quickly than you think.

CHAPTER 14: ABOUT TEACHING

As we've discussed throughout this book, it takes a lot of courage to do the work we do. It takes even more courage to feel qualified to teach. I'm lucky to have had some very wonderful, qualified teachers, and I realize it is now my job to teach. I can take all the things I've learned, both from teachers and in my own practice as a psychic medium, and decide which of the things have resonated enough for me to teach.

A few months after I finished taking my first class for mediums, I had about ten people ask me to teach a class about it before it actually dawned on me that I was supposed to do that. I felt that although there are other mediums where I live, no one was really teaching about being a medium. Plenty of others taught classes about things like psychic development, but I realized that there were other budding mediums that were as frustrated as I was once at not having a teacher. In that first class I taught all those years ago, I wouldn't say I was terrified: I just was amazed that other people also thought that I had something to teach them.

I used to teach almost exactly what I'd been taught in my first class, but as I have learned more over the years, that has evolved. I'm a person who likes minimal structure. It's a challenge for me just to schedule a class, let alone plan it. I have learned that the best practice for me is to write down the things I want to talk about in class beforehand. I do that not only for me, but for the students. As you know, not everyone is comfortable with not having some sort of outline or plan for what is going to happen.

When I teach, it's not solely a lecture. It, of course, depends on the class, but the only way you really learn or get practice is by doing the work. Because of that, I encourage my students to work by trying readings with each other in a group. That way they can try to apply what they've learned and have a teacher and other students to support them.

I typically keep my classes to four to six hours on one day during a weekend with a lunch break in the middle of the day. The day goes very fast.

During a typical class, we follow a pretty standard routine.

- We start with introductions; everyone talks about why they are there.
- I typically speak about what we are going to learn to do. I usually also explain that it's possible we may slightly change directions because I let Spirit guide me in classes.
- I normally start with a psychic exercise and don't start medium work until after lunch.
- We talk about readings, including what the difference between medium and psychic readings are and why they are both important because all mediums are also psychic.
- We talk about the elements of a reading, and then we practice.

- I first split them into pairs to do readings on each other. I go around and coach each pair as needed.

At the end of class, sometimes I encourage my students to sit in circle and have one person in the center that does a live audience reading. It's scary for them, but they came to class to learn. It usually turns out well. Students get to see how others work, and we can coach each other and learn from each other at the same time. Of course, as the teacher, I can help if it's needed while they read. Then, at the end of the reading, we may talk about it as a group.

There are two group exercises I often use in class.

- Sitting for Names: We spend a few minutes writing any name that comes to our head and then call them off one-by-one to the group. The members of the group must then raise their hands to claim their respective dead person. Not all of the names get picked, of course, but many times they do, even the odd names. It's a good exercise to give some confidence to beginner students.
- Psychic Keyhole: I usually mention a room in my house or have someone volunteer to mention a room in their home. Then, for a few minutes, we all write down the things that we see in the room.

There are many other types of classes you can teach. You could teach a class that is solely a psychic development series. You can teach a class about something else you know about such as chakras or angels. You could also think about teaching an online class, which may get you a wider audience. I also used to work with a peer to lead a support group of sorts, a place that anyone could stop on their journey in all things metaphysical.

If you think that it's a challenge to give a public reading, it may also be a challenge for you to teach. If public speaking itself is a challenge or scary for you, there are wonderful organizations such as Toastmasters International that can truly help those who want to develop the courage or experience to do well at public speaking.

There are many students that need qualified teachers. That does not mean you have to be world famous or have tons of experience. Perhaps, you may have a small bit of experience that you can share with others. Personally, I believe it's my duty to take what I've learned and teach people that knowledge. Not everyone has had the resources I've had, nor do they have the communication style I do. Not only do I want to be the best I can be at giving readings, I also want to always strive to be a better teacher.

If you have felt any inclination to or have been asked by several people to teach, it may be time to take that leap of faith and schedule a class and market it to the people who might want to take it. At some point, when you feel like you've learned enough or have something to share that could benefit others, pay it forward and teach the things you were once taught to the new generation of people that are trying to learn more so they can do this work.

CHAPTER 15: ABOUT WRITING

There are many of you out there that may have already thought of writing. Some of you think this is applies to anyone but you, but hear me out just in case there's a book, a blog, or any sort of helpful writing in your future.

I first started writing when I was 14. I grew up during the days before there was any sort of Young Adult fiction books like they have now for young adults, and I wanted to write my own take on the things out there. For a while, I wanted to be (and was) a songwriter. I started writing a blog, and you can still many of the articles that I first wrote on my website (http://www.lisaandres.com).

Still, when I had a prophetic dream that was a near death experience in 2012 that commanded me to write a book, it was surreal. I saw my soul float out of my body and the gold light that led upwards beside my bed. The energy I felt outside my body was like a love and peace I'd never known, and my automatic reaction was to follow it. Alas, it must not have been my time because I declared to whomever might be listening "But I'm not ready to go." To this, I heard a very authoritative voice say, "Then write the book."

"What book?" was my immediate thought. After that, I popped back into reality and resolved to write a book, only I didn't know what to write. I'd always wanted to write fiction, but since I had experience at that time already working as a psychic medium, I remembered all the things I had wanted to know along my journey but had not yet found in books.

By the time I first sat down to write, I still was somewhat of a skeptic about this writing thing. I didn't think I'd be any good at it, as well as all the other things anyone would say to themselves about writing. The thought of writing an entire book was daunting, and I wasn't sure what to do or how to do it. At that point, I thought about the metaphysical classes I had taught and what I had covered when I had tutored students, and I decided to make a list of subjects that I thought might be interesting to people reading. I also asked the followers of my Lisa Andres Psychic Medium Facebook page (https://www.facebook.com/lisajandres/) what I should put in the book and what they wanted to hear about. One suggestion turned into the "Spirit Guides" chapter. I also wrote the first chapter, "My Story," after that because my own spirit guides said people would want to know who I was and how I got to where I was at that point.

I wrote one chapter at a time, but they didn't take the form of chapters in the beginning. I wrote about the things that I knew. One subject, such as past lives, went into one Microsoft Word document and another topic would go into its own file. I wrote while I had a full-time job during the day for about a year, here and there, as I felt guided. At one point, I let the book sit for a couple of months until I got back from a class with other mediums, which just gave me a bit more insight into what I had already written about doing medium readings. I got to the point where I felt done contributing anything new to the manuscript, but I somehow intuitively knew the book wasn't done.

Therefore, I asked my guides what I should do and went with what I felt.

Then, voila, the book was done. Before it was released, I had all sorts of fears about it like "Who am I to be doing this?" and "What will my peers think?" Despite those fears, I self-published my book with the thought that as long as I helped one person, then it was all worthwhile. That book is now *Gifted – A Guide for Mediums, Psychics & Intuitives*. Since then, the book has had a life of its own, and it has continually sold since it was released in 2013. That tells me two things. I have a voice that people can relate to on this subject and, more so, that there's not enough of this type of material out there. That also means that there is an audience out there that could be looking for YOU and your voice.

After that book launched, my editors sent a note to their clients wanting short stories for an anthology. That inspired an idea in me to write a Christmas romance. At that point, it was early September, and if I wanted to get a novella out for Christmas, I had to do it fast. I had ideas, but I asked my angels for help. The next morning I woke up with the idea for the book that is now *Dubicki's* by Gabriella Scott (my pen name for romance).

My first romance woke something in me. It was so fun writing and getting to know my characters. I wanted to see how the story finished, so I just kept writing until it was done.

I knew when I published it that the fiction readers would not be quite as polite as the audience that read *Gifted*. They were so honest I had a good cry or two, but a few did give me some tips. After that, I went to a class or two about writing, and I eventually published another book in that series.

I look back and realize that some of it was rushed, and, a few books in at this point, what I have learned is that writing does not have to be rushed. It's good to have goals, but it's better for me personally if I don't force writing and don't stop my life for writing. It's all in the intention, so if you think you'd never have the time or talent to write a book, think again. I was a music major, not an English major.

Having fiction books out there is more of a hobby at this point, but I do intend to continue to build that brand and keep writing fiction because I love it. I joined a romance writing group where I live, as well as the Romance Writers of America, and I will continue to develop that side of my writing.

With non-fiction material about the metaphysical world, as I said, there are not enough of us out there writing. There's no recipe on how to do it. You just need to have the desire to help people and then sit down to write every once in a while. If you don't know what to write about, ask the universe to help give you clear guided signs or show you the way and then trust that will happen. I see so many of people posting wonderful thoughts or stories about readings on social media, and it would be nice to have that evolve into a book to help others. There are people out there who want to hear what you have to say, including me. I want to read your book!

Self-Publishing

A lot of people ask me about self-publishing, so I would like to at least give you tools the basic tools to get you started.

Basic Tools for Self-Publishing

Hire an editor.

Hiring an editor is a must. You need to hire an actual professional, not your best friend, high school teacher, or the like.

Get a professional cover image.

You will need a professional cover image for your book. There are a lot of premade covers out there you can buy that will likely come out better than a cover design you do yourself via the cover creator on the site you self-publish through (unless you're a graphic designer and that's your thing). Get a wrap cover if you want to publish a paper version, as well as an e-book cover. A wrap cover is for print books and includes the front cover, back cover, and a spine.

Have a professional website.

When people read what you write, they will want to find you on the Internet. You can start with you own cost-effective website. As I've mentioned, I had a WordPress website designed cost-effectively and worked with web designers so I could make payments.

Get it formatted correctly.

You will need your book formatted correctly for submission to whatever website you use to self-publish or for whatever other means that you have it published by. I have my editors do my formatting.

Buy an ISBN.

If you want the book self-published with an imprint of your own name or company rather than having an imprint of CreateSpace, for instance, you will want to purchase your own ISBN. You can obtain one for free from many self-publishing sites if you want to use that imprint and don't care about that detail. I've tried both and like to have my own imprint in the books, so I buy the ISBN for both the print and digital versions of my books. (https://www.myidentifiers.com)

Watch the length of the book.

Do not make the book over 400 pages long. That's too long for most books, and your reader will tend to lose interest or not buy it at all because it's too long.

Market the book.

As I've discussed in this book, you will need to market your book. You can do this by creating a buzz before it's released. As I am writing this book, I am already in the process of doing that with this book. For further reference, revisit Chapter 13 of this book, "The Business Section."

The Real Work with Self-Publishing

The real work with self-publishing is in the writing, which takes effort no matter what. I have been to writers' group with professional writers that say they procrastinate in every way when they write, so I know it's not just me. They, however, use excuses like they have editors that they owe a manuscript to in a week and have to pull all-nighters because they write best under pressure. For now, this is why I like being self-published. I do have to be courteous and coordinate timing with my editors and cover designer, but other than that, I can give myself reasonable deadlines.

Procrastination happens sometimes, but the book will not get written if you don't write it, even if it is just a little at a time. There are times that I write when I start to immediately think what I am writing is awful or I want to throw it out. I force myself to write and get my internal editor out of my head because some of the most authentic things are written that way. If you do feel you need to throw away pages or words, make sure you save them elsewhere. I have a folder I call "The Parking Lot" where things like that go in case I want them later.

There's no wrong way to write, just please consider getting out there and writing whatever your heart desires. If you feel guided to write it, there's someone out there who might need it, and you'll never know unless you try.

BONUS EXCERPT

GIFTED

A Guide for Mediums, Psychics, and Intuitives

Lisa Andres

, in brief, are the different types of clairs (from the French *clair*, meaning "clear"):

- Clairvoyance: The ability to SEE psychic information
- Clairaudience: The ability to HEAR psychic information
- Clairsentience: The ability to FEEL (touch) psychic information
- Claircognizance: The ability to KNOW psychic information (You don't know how you know; you just know it.)
- Clairalience: The ability to SMELL psychic information
- Clairgustance: The ability to obtain psychic information through TASTE

There may be other clairs, but these are the ones I resonate with the most. You may have some of them, or you may have all of them. You may not know if you have any at all. That's okay.

Chances are good that you have more than one of these. I resonate with each of them in some way or the other. The only one I don't recall ever having or using is clairgustance. The one that I resonate with the most is claircognizance. That is: I don't know how I know; I just know it. You may be different and identify with one now, and then find that as you develop your skill set, you find you possess and use many different clairs.

In my early years, I remember a clear sense of clairalience. Every woman in my mother's family has an extraordinary sense of smell; meaning that I have felt at times that my nose rivals a canine's. I have heard many times that psychics have heightened senses, but let's just say that early in life I learned how to hold my nose without touching it and had times I wished I could turn off my extraordinary olfactory perception. Later I learned that this could help me identify departed loved ones. Every time my deceased great grandmother was near, I could smell the soap she used that I associated with her. As time went by, I developed clairaudience. When dead people were near, I could hear voices, coughing, or even whistling.

I'm primarily left-brained (logical and analytical), so it took a while before clairvoyance came into the picture. And when it did, I resisted. When I started to do readings, I had a very specific idea of how it was going to happen and told my guides the left-brained things I'd like to hear (spelled words, numbers, etc.). So, what happened? My guides started to show me pictures, which just *hurt* to try to see at first! I realize, now, they did that just to help me develop my clairvoyance, and now it's second nature to me. When I do readings now, there are many clairs that come into play. I can't say that I'm really thinking about which one it is or is not, I'm just grateful that I have the various clair tools in my chest, so to speak, to help me relay a message to a client.

Clairvoyance evolved into claircognizance. I didn't know where the information was coming from: it just came out in the message I was relaying. Here's a good example of claircognizance: you know how you sometimes get a phone call, and you just knew the person was going to call? That is claircognizance!

You do not have to remember all of these labels. They are just intended as a point of reference for you as you learn. The best way to get this in your own way is to have an idea of what clair you want, have, or don't have. It was not until I got out of my own way and stopped thinking that I had to see or hear things a certain way, that the information started coming to me more freely.

ANGELS

Angels are with you all of the time. You probably have believed that you have a guardian angel for some time, perhaps all of your life. We all have one. The main purpose of a guardian angel is to protect you from an untimely death. Have you had times where you felt you were miraculously saved from some sort of disaster, such as a traffic accident? Well, that was likely the intervention of your guardian angel.

What you may not know is that there are several angels around you at all times. They would love to help you with anything and everything. As humans, part of our contract on Earth is that we have free will to make our own choices during this life on Earth. What that means is that angels cannot intervene unless we ask. They love to help us, if only we ask. Now, that does not always mean you will get an instant answer, or the answer that you want, but they will always help when you actually ask.

Angels come with only love and are without judgment of any sort. Most of them have never had human lives and work for God. So, if you have ever thought an angel was telling you something such as "You're bad," it wasn't an angel. Most likely that was an ego-based thought from a place of fear.

If you want to ask an angel for help, you can ask either out loud or in your head. They love it when you talk to them and tell them all your problems or your fears and desires. You can never tell them too much or too little. They are with you at all times.

There are times when I say to mine, "Please take my fears about this situation (that is troubling me)."

I imagine myself lifting my arms and giving my burden to the angels. I had a broken heart a few years ago, and I knew I would be filled with sorrow and grief while I healed. Since the pain of heartbreak is so excruciating, I asked my angels to please take some of my sadness from me. I have always felt that they did.

Prior to my realization and acceptance of being a medium and a psychic, I was feeling a bit like a victim. I did not understand why I was on Earth, and I felt cynical about many things. As I drove to work one day, I was singing along to a song by Sara Bareilles called "Come Round Soon." I was singing her lyrics at the top of my lungs, "The angels said I'd smile today. Who needs angels anyway?"

I remember thinking, "Yeah, it's not like they've ever helped me anyway!"

A few months later, I received a book about angels as a gift, and it changed my life. Not only do I now believe in angels, I ask for their help in many things. When you see sparkles or mysterious flashes of color in the air around you, usually above the head, those are angels. When you see colored sparkles of light in the air, it is usually an Archangel. When you see sparkles of white light, they represent other angels such as guardian angels or angels that are with or near you.

Clients I give readings to often ask, "What angel do I have with me?" This is likely something you will get in your practice, as well. As with any reading, it is the first thing that pops into my head or first thing that I intuit. So, if I feel that it is Archangel Michael, I may say, "I feel that you have a strong connection to Archangel Michael. He is associated with the color purple. Is purple one of your favorite colors? Do you sometimes notice that you just manifest purple things around you? You might even see purple flecks or sparkles in the air at times."

The answer is almost always "yes" when that is the information I feel guided to provide. So, if you see a color that you LOVE, have everywhere, wear often, or see, possibly as the colored sparkles in the air, it is likely the archangel that you associate with most. My Grandma Ali loves, loves, loves the color purple, so what does that say about her? She has probably got Archangel Michael with her! The angels want to remind you that you can call on them anytime, for anything. No request is too big or too small. You do not have to worry about taking an archangel, or any angel, away from someone else who needs them more. Angels are omnipresent, meaning they can be with many people simultaneously.

Remember, when you ask them for assistance, you may not always receive an immediate answer. Also, they may not always answer in the way you think they should answer. The trick is to try to let go of the details and the need to understand how something is going to happen, and let it transpire with the help of the angels. You then have to trust that it will happen. The angels hear you the first time you ask, and they usually are not expecting you to ask them again. At times, it may seem like you are not receiving an answer, but it may be that your desire has not yet manifested. It is also possible that no answer, or what you perceive to be no answer, is, in fact, the answer that is for your highest good. You just may not realize it at the time, or it could be that more patience is required. Regardless, your requests to the angels do not go unanswered. It just may not be the outcome you expect.

If you want a sign that your angel is there, ask for a sign. Angels sometimes give signs in the form of coins. If you see one that is on the ground, it is usually a sign from an angel. A sign from an angel is proof of their love and that they are near you. The same can be said of feathers. Even if it is a feather from something in your home such as a down coat or pillow, it is a sign from an angel. At times, I see a vehicle pass me with a business name that has "angel" in the title or a school bus with "angel" in the name of the school. I always know that represents a sign from the angels.

Certain songs contain messages from angels. Whenever I hear these songs, I know it is a sign from my angels. In 2010, I was moving across the country (1,400 miles) to Boston, Massachusetts. When I was looking for an apartment in Boston, I was crushed for time since I was only there for a weekend. I also did not know the neighborhoods. I did not know if I would find the right place, and I was worried about it. I drove to a new neighborhood my realtor had suggested, and it felt good to me. I grew up in a Jewish neighborhood and saw a synagogue on the corner. I knew that was a sign because it made me feel at home. Then, all of the sudden, a song that I associate as being an angel message came on the radio. It had never really had radio play, yet there it was playing on my radio. I knew it was a sign from my angels, and, even though I had not pulled up to the apartment, I could not help wondering if this would be my home. Sure enough, I ended up signing a lease for that apartment, and I always knew that my angels helped me find it.

So, if you ask your angels for a sign, try to stay open and be receptive to the answer. If you hear a song and say, "I wonder if that's from my angels," it is. If you see something and wonder if that is the sign you were looking for, it is. That's your intuition telling you that it is, along with your angels. Sometimes, I see signs at random from angels when I am having a bad or dark-seeming day. One day I was rather cranky on my way to work, wondering WHY on Earth I had this long commute and had to sit in traffic, etc. As I was sitting there at a stoplight, all of the sudden, a school bus pulled up beside me that said *Academy of Holy Angels* on the side. I started to cry happy tears and knew it was a message of love and support from the angels.

One practice I have recently adopted is to ask the angels at bedtime to rearrange my thoughts so that my dreams will work to my greatest and highest good. It is important to know that you should be sober when you do this. I always wake up the next morning feeling refreshed, like I have been cleansed in a special way.

You have an extra special connection to the angels if you are always inspired to put angel-themed decor in your home or work place. If you have a tattoo of wings, you are probably part angel yourself. Remember when I said that a lightworker is also known as an Earth angel? Well, Earth angels can be part angel or have angel-like qualities. If your name is Angel, Angela, or something with "angel" in it, you definitely have a connection to angels.

Your angels are full of love for you and always by your side. They love that you are reading this and that you want to know more about angels. Just remember, your angels are only a thought away. You do not need to know who they are to ask for their help. You do not need to be Christian, or any other religion for that matter, to ask for their help. They love everyone, as they all see everyone as Love.

They are waiting for you to ask for their assistance. If you are afraid to ask, just start by thanking them for being there. You do not have to see them to do that. You can start by asking them to come to you in your dreams. You can also ask them to protect you, your house, or your loved ones at any time. Whatever it is you want to ask, there is nothing too big or too small, just ask. Even if you are not yet ready to ask them for anything, take comfort in knowing that there are always angels around us.

Archangels

Archangels are, in many ways, an extension of the hand of God. They work to carry our prayers to God and also to dispatch teams of even more angels to help answer our prayers. There are more archangels than the ones in this section, but these are the ones I felt guided to share with you and work with most often. I am listing them as a resource for you so that you can know who they are and what their specialties are. As with any angel, you may call on them for anything. This resource may help point you in the right direction if you do not know where to start.

Archangel Michael – Protector

Archangel Michael is the universal, or all-purpose, archangel. He shields and protects all who ask, and he has contracted with some to come as part of their spiritual team. He is often associated with police officers and any additional civil servants who protect others. He is with the Indigos, as they are warriors of some sort who effect positive change. He is also a wonderful resource for technology and issues that need a fix of some sort, such as help with your computer or a plumbing fix.

He also works to protect mediums, especially if they are "ghost busting." He can dispatch a squadron to help a lost soul heal and cross over to the light.

Color: Purple/Cobalt Blue

You can ask Archangel Michael to guard you at all times in all relationships and aspects of your life. He will make sure that you are safe. He wants you to know, however, if you do this, you may also lose some relationships or situations in your life that are not for your greatest and highest good. These relationships may or may not re-enter your life at a time when they are better suited for your greatest good. In many instances, his intervention helps to align your energy with those that compliment it the most, and it can also bring wonderful new relationships and situations into your life, as well.

Archangel Raphael – Healer

Archangel Raphael has green healing energy, and he is present with those that need healing or are healers. He is present on the spiritual team with all doctors and healers, whether traditional or non-traditional healers. He is also present with Crystal adults and children.

Color: Emerald Green

You can ask Archangel Raphael for healing for yourself or others that need help. You can send him to a person, even if you do not necessarily have their actual consent or knowledge, with the intention of Raphael healing the person with their soul's permission.

Archangel Gabriel – Messenger

Archangel Gabriel is the Messenger of God. He is present with all orators, whether they are involved with the spoken or written word. If you are an author or musician that creates books or music, for instance, Gabriel is with you. If you are someone that speaks to crowds in an inspirational way, Gabriel is with you. Call upon him if you wish to have a child, whether through conception or adoption. He is also present with many children. This includes crystal children and some of the Indigos.

Color: Silver and/or Gold

You can call upon Archangel Gabriel if you are looking for inspiration in your career as an author. Even if you have not started the book or work yet, he will inspire you with divine guidance, helping you successfully complete your project or reach your desired result.

Archangel Jophiel – Beauty

Archangel Jophiel is helpful when you need to call upon her to beautify your home, wardrobe, appearance, or thoughts. She is also a wonderful resource for clearing energy in homes. If you clear homes in any way, such as with Feng Shui, interior design, or even in helping clear earthbound spirits from homes, call upon Archangel Jophiel for help.

Color: Hot Pink

You can call on Archangel Jophiel to clear your thoughts. In instances where you worry excessively or want to clear the energy from a disagreement you may have had with someone, ask Jophiel for assistance and allow yourself to relax as she clears your energy.

Archangel Azrael – Death, Dying, Grief

Archangel Azrael is sometimes thought of as the angel of death. It is not something to fear because death is a necessary part of our existence on Earth. Archangel Azrael is always amongst the spiritual teams of mediums, hospice workers, funeral directors, and anyone that assists in the physical death process, whether it is before or after death. He also assists with grief of any kind, whether from the death of a person or relationship of any kind.

I received affirmation that I had Archangel Azrael with me when I went back to Corporate America and got a job working on death settlements in the financial services industry. I already knew I was a medium, but the synchronicity is that I help dead people whether it is in a traditional or non-traditional way. The affirmation of that in my structured job was not a coincidence.

Color: Ecru

You can call on Archangel Azrael if you are grieving a loved one, whether it is a recent loss or not. If you have experienced heartbreak in your life, call on Archangel Azrael to assist you and take some of the grief.

Archangel Ariel – Animals, Environment

Archangel Ariel has the face of a Lion because she is known as the Lioness of God. Ask for her assistance with any issue pertaining to an animal. She can help you find the right animal to adopt or help with things such as behavior issues with animals in your life. She cares for our Earth's environment and is particularly close to anyone that feels called to work on environmental issues.

Color: Light Pink

If you feel connected to faeries and wish to see them or know they are there, ask Archangel Ariel for help in doing so. You will receive the answers in the form of thoughts, feelings, and synchronicities regarding faeries. The fairies are connected to the outdoors, and so is Archangel Ariel.

Archangel Nathaniel – Life Changes

Archangel Nathaniel has been very present with all the lightworkers experiencing life changes. He has had more presence on Earth recently, with all the vast changes that have been happening in our lives, whether good or bad. Some of these changes come to help us towards our life purpose. Archangel Nathaniel is here to help us with that transition.

I did not know that this was an archangel I had near me until I realized that one of my favorite colors is red. I have a red car, red phone, red jacket, you name it. I have also experienced many life changes, particularly recently.

Color: Red

Call upon Archangel Nathaniel to assist with the ease in transition during your life changes. If you feel that it has been hard, tell him and ask for his assistance. If you want a life change, such as career better suited to your life purpose, ask him.

Archangel Metatron – Akashic Records, Children

Archangel Metatron is one of two archangels who lived as mortals before becoming archangels. On Earth, he was known as the profit Enoch. He has now ascended to the heavens to continue his work as a scribe by recording all of the information in and for the Akashic records. Metatron is also present on the spiritual team of all Indigo children and adults, and he is a helper to anyone that wishes to teach children for the greatest and highest good of all involved.

Color: Turquoise Blue/Green

Ask Archangel Metatron for help if you want to balance your chakras. He can do so with his sacred geometry. He starts balancing your chakras on the top of your head, with a sphere-shaped energy that contains the sacred geometry used to achieve balance.

Archangel Sandalphon – Answered Prayers, Music

Archangel Sandalphon is one of two archangels that lived as mortals before ascending to Heaven as archangels. As a

one of the main overseers of the Akashic records. Call upon him to access esoteric information and for help with alchemy and manifestation.

Color: Plum (dark purple)

Call upon Archangel Raziel if you feel guided to work with Akashic records in any way or if you need help remembering a piece of your life purpose. He will guide to you the esoteric secrets in your soul and help you remember and apply divine manifestation principles in your life.

Archangel Raguel – Fairness and Harmony

Archangel Raguel's name means "Friend of God". He oversees all the relationships between archangels and angels. He helps add balance and harmony to relationships, and he is known for helping restore justice for the greatest and highest good of all in something such as a legal proceeding.

Color: Orange

Call upon Archangel Raguel to help in balancing drama in current relationships and also to find new relationships that will be for you greatest and highest good and add harmony to your life.

Archangel Jeremiel – Life Review

Archangel Jeremiel's name means "Mercy of God". He often helps others review their life, whether it is a new soul that has crossed over from Earth or to help us access memories in our past from which we can learn and grow.

Color: Dark Yellow

Call upon Archangel Jeremiel to assist with a current life review to help you with your life purpose.

NOTES

NOTES

<u>NOTES</u>

NOTES

ABOUT THE AUTHOR

Lisa Andres has been a psychic medium all her life and has been doing readings for others since 2007.She has a background on the stage because her first dream in life was to be a rock star, but life had other plans for her. Now she works with Spirit to bring through the evidence and messages that only loved ones on the other side can provide. With Lisa's unique style, she articulates the messages that Spirit brings through in a way that no one else can. She does private sittings, as well as events, parties, and live audience readings, which are one of the things she does best.

Lisa has had many teachers, and now she teaches students both in-person and through her books. Her first book, *Gifted – A Guide for Mediums, Psychics and Intuitives*, was released in 2013. Her most recent book, *Journey – The Gift of Being a Psychic Medium*, was released in 2018.

OTHER BOOKS BY LISA ANDRES

*Gifted – A Guide for Mediums, Psychics, &
Intuitives*

*Indigo Warrior – A Guide for Indigo Adults and the
Parents of Indigo Children*

LISA ANDRES